DK First
SPAN‌ISH
Picture Dictionary

Contents

LONDON, NEW YORK, MUNICH,
MELBOURNE, and DELHI

Senior Editors
Hannah Wilson, Julie Ferris

Project Editor Anna Harrison

Editor Elise See Tai

Art Editors
Ann Cannings, Emy Manby

U.S. Editor Elizabeth Hester

DTP Designer David McDonald

Production Harriet Maxwell

Translator Candy Rodó

Managing Editor
Scarlett O'Hara

First American Edition, 2005
First Scholastic paperback edition 2005

First published in the United States by
DK Publishing, Inc.
375 Hudson Street
New York, New York 10014

06 07 08 10 9 8 7 6 5 4 3
Copyright © 2005, Dorling Kindersley Ltd

A Cataloging-in-Publication record for this book
is available from the Library of Congress.

ISBN-13 978-0-7566-1370-9 (hb)
ISBN-10 0-7566-1370-1 (hb)
ISBN-13 978-0-7566-1939-8 (pb)
ISBN-10 0-7566-1939-4 (pb)

Color reproduction by Colourscan, Singapore
Printed and bound in China by SNP Leefung

Discover more at **www.dk.com**

How to use this dictionary

Find out how you can get the most from your dictionary. At the beginning of the book, there are Topic pages. These include lots of useful words on a particular subject, such as *Pets* and *In the Park*. Each word has its translation and help with how to pronounce it. The words on the Topic pages can be found in the English A–Z and in the Spanish A–Z. There are lots of other useful words here too. The verbs and a pronunciation guide are in another section. At the back of the book, there is a list of useful phrases for you to practice your Spanish with your friends.

Topic pages

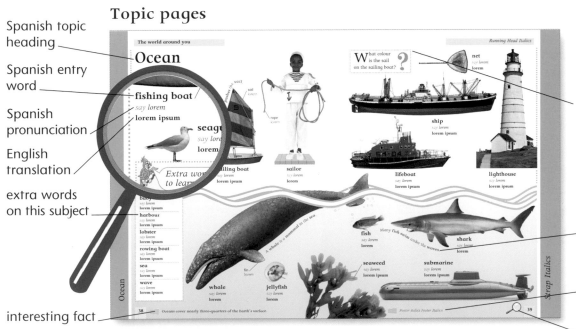

Spanish topic heading

Spanish entry word

Spanish pronunciation

English translation

extra words on this subject

interesting fact

translation of topic heading

question for language practice

simple sentence with topic vocabulary

translation of interesting fact

English to Spanish A–Z

first word on the page with the Spanish translation

English entry word

Spanish translation

Spanish pronunciation

last word on the page with the Spanish translation

first letter of the words on the page

Look for me on the topic pages!

Acerca de mí

All about me

Soy alta.

el hermano
air-MAH-noh
brother

la hermana
air-MAH-nah
sister

el bebé
beh-BEH
baby

el padre
PAH-dray
father

la madre
MAH-dray
mother

Ésta es mi familia.

el abuelo
grandfather

la abuela
grandmother

los abuelos
ah-BOO'AY-los
grandparents

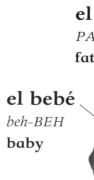

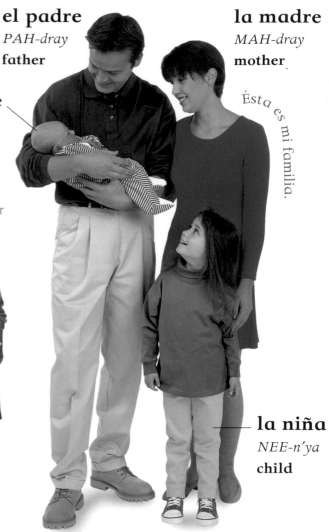

la niña
NEE-n'ya
child

la tía
TEE-ah
aunt

el tío
TEE-o
uncle

¡Somos felices!

feliz
fay-LEES
happy

Tom está enfadado.

enfadado
en-fah-DAH-do
angry

4 ¡Tu cuerpo tiene unos 206 huesos!

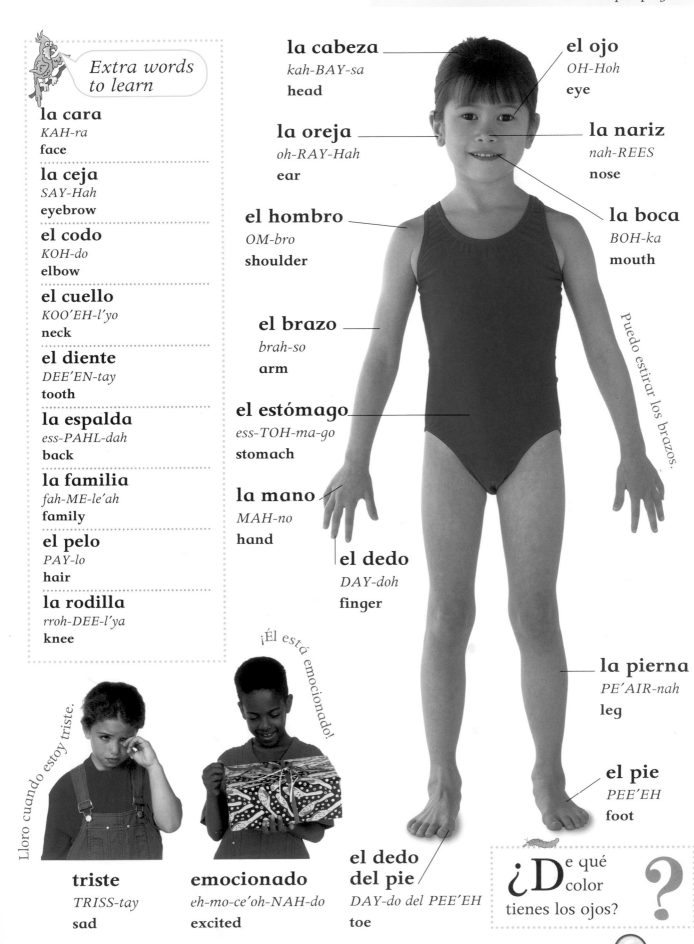

Extra words to learn

la cara
KAH-ra
face

la ceja
SAY-Hah
eyebrow

el codo
KOH-do
elbow

el cuello
KOO'EH-l'yo
neck

el diente
DEE'EN-tay
tooth

la espalda
ess-PAHL-dah
back

la familia
fah-ME-le'ah
family

el pelo
PAY-lo
hair

la rodilla
rroh-DEE-l'ya
knee

la cabeza
kah-BAY-sa
head

el ojo
OH-Hoh
eye

la oreja
oh-RAY-Hah
ear

la nariz
nah-REES
nose

el hombro
OM-bro
shoulder

la boca
BOH-ka
mouth

el brazo
brah-so
arm

el estómago
ess-TOH-ma-go
stomach

la mano
MAH-no
hand

el dedo
DAY-doh
finger

Puedo estirar los brazos.

la pierna
PE'AIR-nah
leg

el pie
PEE'EH
foot

Lloro cuando estoy triste.

¡Él está emocionado!

triste
TRISS-tay
sad

emocionado
eh-mo-ce'oh-NAH-do
excited

el dedo del pie
DAY-do del PEE'EH
toe

¿**D**e qué color tienes los ojos?

There are about 206 bones in your body!

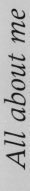

All about me

5

La ropa
Clothes

el botón
button

la camisa
la camisa
ka-MEE-sa
shirt

los calcetines
kal-say-TEE-nays
socks

los vaqueros
bah-KAY-ros
jeans

Extra words to learn

las gafas
GAH-fas
glasses

el guante
goo'AN-tay
glove

el pijama
pee-HAH-ma
pajamas

la ropa interior
RRO-pa in-tay-RE'OR
underwear

el suéter
SOO'EH-tair
sweater

el vestido
behs-TE-do
dress

la zapatilla
sa-pa-TEE-l'ya
slipper

el zapato
sa-pah-to
shoe

la cremallera
zipper

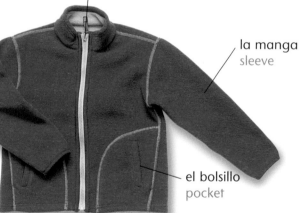

la manga
sleeve

el bolsillo
pocket

el forro polar
FOR-rro po-LAR
fleece

la bufanda
boo-FAHN-da
scarf

el guante
glove

Mi abrigo me mantiene calentita.

el abrigo
ah-BREE-go
coat

las zapatillas deportivas
sa-pah-tee-yahs day-por-TEE-bas
sneakers

La ropa

¡Los vaqueros tienen más de 130 años!

el cinturón
belt

los pantalones cortos
pan-ta-LOH-ness KOR-tos
shorts

el traje de baño
TRAH-Hay day BAH-n'yo
swimsuit

la camiseta
ka-mee-SAY-ta
T-shirt

los pantalones
pan-ta-LOH-ness
pants

la chaqueta
chah-KAY-ta
jacket

la capucha
hood

la falda
FAHL-da
skirt

el chubasquero
choo-bas-KAY-roh
raincoat

los vaqueros
jeans

Los vaqueros y las zapatillas son mi ropa favorita.

las botas
BO-tahs
boots

¿Te gusta llevar zapatos o zapatillas deportivas?

Jeans are more than 130 years old!

Clothes

La cocina
Kitchen

el cazo
saucepan

el horno
oven

la sartén
sar-TAYN
frying pan

el plato
PLAH-to
plate

la cocina
ko-SEE-na
stove

la cuchara
koo-CHAH-ra
spoon

la taza
TAH-sa
mug

el libro
book

el paño de cocina
PAH-n'yo day ko-SEE-na
dish towel

el tazón
tah-SON
bowl

el cazo
KAH-so
saucepan

¿**Q**ué hay en la cuchara?

8 La primera cocina de gas se fabricó en 1826.

Gracias por lavar los platos.

la alacena
cupboard

el fregadero

fray-ga-DEH-ro

sink

el congelador
freezer

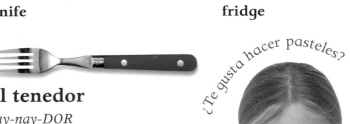

el refrigerador

reh-free-Hay-ra-DOR

fridge

*Extra words
to learn*

la bandeja
ban-DAY-Hah
tray

el cubo de la basura
KOO-bo deh lah bah-SOO-rah
trash can

el hervidor
air-BE-dor
kettle

la jarra
HAR-rrah
jug

la lavadora
la-ba-DO-ra
washing machine

la plancha
PLAN-chah
iron

la taza
TAH-sa
cup

la tostadora
toss-ta-DOR-ra
toaster

el cuchillo
koo-CHEE-l'yo
knife

el tenedor
tay-nay-DOR
fork

¿Te gusta hacer pasteles?

el delantal
day-lahn-TAHL
apron

la manopla
mah-NO-plah
oven mitt

el vaso
BAH-so
glass

The first gas stove was made in 1826.

Kitchen

El baño

Bathroom

el peine
PAY'EN-neh
comb

el baño
BAHN-n'yo
bath

el agua
ah-GOO'AH
water

el juguete
Hoo-GAY-tay
toy

Pongo pasta de dientes en mi cepillo de dientes.

la esponja
es-PON-Hah
sponge

las toallas
to-AH-l'yas
towels

el tubo
tube

la pasta de dientes
PASS-ta day DEE'EN-tess
toothpaste

el cepillo de dientes
say-PEE-l'yo day DEE'EN-tess
toothbrush

¿Cuántas cosas amarillas hay en esta página?

 ¡El baño más caro del mundo tiene un inodoro de oro!

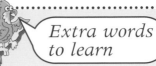

el champú
cham-POO
shampoo

el espejo
ess-PAY-Ho
mirror

el cepillo de pelo
say-PE-l'yo day PAY-lo
hairbrush

el enchufe
en-choo-fay
plug

el maquillaje
mah-kee-L'YAH-Heh
make-up

el paño
PAH-n'yo
washcloth

los pañuelos de papel
pah-N'YU'AL-los day pah-PELL
tissues

el vapor
BAH-por
steam

la ducha
DOO-chah
shower

el papel higiénico
pah-PELL ee-HAY-nee-ko
toilet paper

el jabón
Hah-BON
soap

el inodoro
ee-no-DOH-ro
toilet

el grifo
GREE-fo
faucet

el paño
washcloth

el jabón
soap

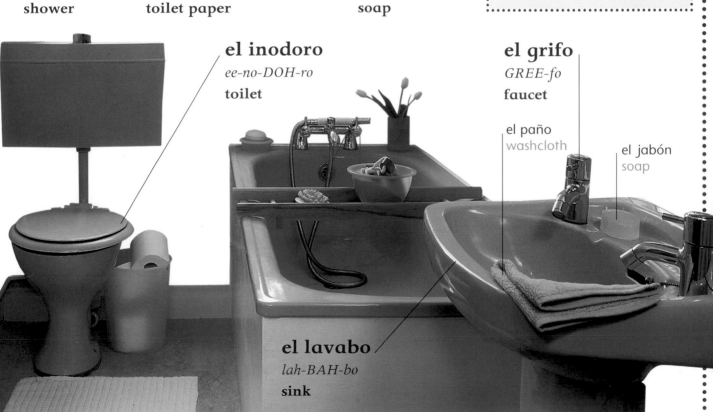

el lavabo
lah-BAH-bo
sink

The world's most expensive bathroom has a gold toilet!

el reloj
rray-loH
clock

la cama
KAH-mah
bed

la almohada
al-moh-AH-da
pillow

el edredón
ay-dray-DON
comforter

la silla
SEE-l'yah
chair

Mi dormitorio
My bedroom

la cómoda
KO-mo-dah
chest of drawers

Duermo en mi cama.

el videojuego
BEE-day-oh-HOO'AY-go
video game

Jugamos a juegos de tablero.

el ajedrez
chess

la alfombra
ahl-FOM-brah
carpet

Mi gato duerme debajo de mi cama.

¿Qué hay dentro del armario?

La alfombra es azul.

Puedo tocar la guitarra.

el tapete
tah-PAY-tay
rug

los libros
LEE-bros
books

el armario
ahr-MAR-re'o
wardrobe

la guitarra
ghee-TAH-rrah
guitar

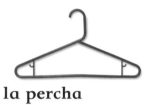

la percha
PER-chah
coat hanger

la lámpara
LAM-pah-rah
lamp

el espejo
ess-PAY-Ho
mirror

13

El jardín
Garden

la carretilla
ka-rray-TEE-l'ya
wheelbarrow

el árbol
AHR-bol
tree

el tronco
trunk

el rastrillo
rrahs-TREE-l'yo
rake

el banco
BAHN-ko
bench

la hierba
YAIR-ba
grass

el cortacésped
kor-tah-SESS-payd
lawn mower

Extra words to learn

el bulbo
BOOL-boh
bulb

la cerca
SAYR-kah
fence

el césped
SESS-payd
lawn

el desplantador
dess-plahn-tah-DOR
trowel

la hoja
Oh-Hah
leaf

el invernadero
in-vair-nah-DAY-ro
greenhouse

la jardinera
Hahr-dee-NAY-rah
gardener

la regadera
ray-ga-DAY-ra
watering can

Normalmente las mariposas vuelan durante el día y las polillas vuelan por la noche.

¿**D**e qué color es la mariquita de esta página? **?**

la concha
shell

el caracol
ka-ra-KOHL
snail

el gusano
goo-SAH-no
worm

el ala
wing

la mariposa
mah-re-PO-sah
butterfly

la abeja
ah-BAY-Hah
bee

la semilla
say-MEE-l'ya
seed

la mariquita
mah-ree-KEE-ta
ladybug

Las flores crecen en el jardín.

María está cavando en el jardín.

la flor
FLOR
flower

la oruga
o-ROO-gah
caterpillar

la tierra
TE'AY-rrah
soil

la pala
PAH-lah
spade

Usually butterflies fly in the day and moths fly at night.

Garden

En la ciudad

In the city

la casa

KAH-sah

house

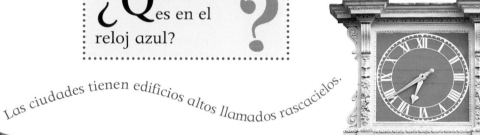

el autobús

ah'oo-to-BOOSS

bus

¿**Q**ué hora es en el reloj azul?

el rascacielos

rass-ka-SEE'AY-los

skyscraper

Las ciudades tienen edificios altos llamados rascacielos.

el reloj

rray-LOH

clock

los apartamentos

ah-par-tah-MEN-tos

apartments

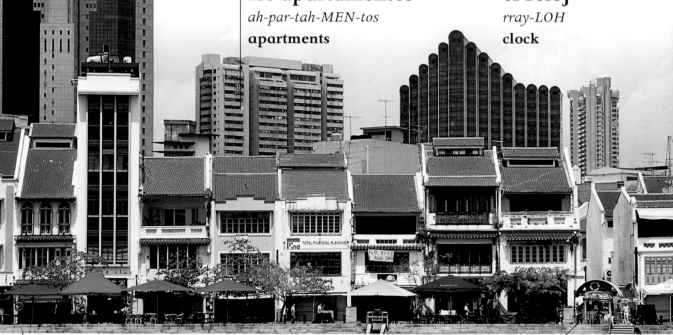

la calle

KAH-l'ye

street

la tienda

tee'ayn-da

shop

Tokio, la capital de Japón, es una de las ciudades más grandes del mundo.

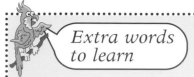
Extra words to learn

el auto
AH'OO-toh
car

la autopista
ah'oo-to-PEES-tah
highway

el banco
BAHN-ko
bank

el café
ka-FAY
café

la fábrica
FAH-bre-kah
factory

el metro
MAY-tro
subway

la parada del autobús
pah-RAH-dah del ah'oo-to-BOOSS
bus stop

el pavimento
pah-be-MEN-to
sidewalk

el teléfono
tay-LAY-fo-no
phone

la señal
say-N'YAL
sign

el semáforo
say-MAH-for-ro
traffic lights

la luz
LOOS
light

el cine
SEE-nay
cinema

el cruce
KROO-say
crossing

el taxi
TAK-see
taxi

el hotel
oh-TEL
hotel

Tokyo, the capital of Japan, is one of the biggest cities in the world.

la cometa
ko-MAY-ta
kite

**la cuerda
de saltar**
*KOO'AIR-da
day sal-TAR*
jump rope

el monopatín
mo-no-pa-TEEN
skateboard

las flores
FLOR-es
flowers

la rueda
RROO'AY-dah
roundabout

En el parque
In the park

¡Me encanta saltar!

la niña
NEE-n'ya
girl

Tres niños juegan en la rueda.

18

Los pájaros hacen ruido.

el árbol
AHR-bol
tree

el columpio
ko-LOOM-pe'oh
swing

el niño
NEE-n'yoh
boy

el balón de fútbol
pah-LON day foot-bol
soccer ball

Mi juego favorito es el fútbol.

la mariposa
mah-re-PO-sa
butterfly

el pájaro
PAH-Hah-ro
bird

la bicicleta
be-se-KLAY-tah
bicycle

la hoja
OH-Hah
leaf

la hierba
YAIR-ba
grass

19

Los pasatiempos
Hobbies

Estoy lista para ir a nadar.

Mis flores crecen.

la acampada
ah-kahn-PAH-do
camping

la natación
na-ta-SE'ON
swimming

la jardinería
Hahr-dee-nay-REE-ah
gardening

observar los pájaros
ob-sair-BAR loss PAH-Hah-ross
bird-watching

Daniela practica cada día.

tocar un instrumento
toh-kar oon in-stroo-MEN-to
playing an instrument

bailar
bah'e-lar
dancing

El surf empezó en Hawaii hace unos 300 años.

Extra words to learn

actuar
ahk-too-AHR
acting

cantar
kan-TAR
singing

el ciclismo
see-KLEES-moh
cycling

cocinar
ko-se-NAR
cooking

coleccionar
ko-lek-se'oh-NAHR
collecting

el dibujo
dee-BOO-ho
drawing

la lectura
lek-TOO-ra
reading

el patinaje en línea
pa-TE-na-Hay en LEE-nee'ah
inline skating

¿Cuál es tu pasatiempo favorito?

hacer surf
ah-SAIR SOORF
surfing

En gimnasia, me estiro y salto.

la gimnasia
Heem-NAH-se'ah
gymnastics

sacar fotos
sah-KAR FOH-toss
taking photos

la pintura
peen-TOO-rah
painting

la escritura
ess-kree-TOO-ra
writing

Surfing began in Hawaii about 300 years ago.

La comida

Food

la naranja

nah-RAHN-Hah

orange

la manzana

mahn-SAH-nah

apple

la semilla
seed

la sandía

san-DEE-a

watermelon

la piel
skin

el plátano

PLAH-tah-no

banana

el tomate

to-MAH-te

tomato

la zanahoria

sah-nah-O-re'ah

carrot

la lechuga

lay-CHOO-gah

lettuce

la col

KOL

cabbage

¡Comemos espaguetis!

el plato
plate

el vaso
glass

el cuchillo
knife

el tenedor
fork

la silla
chair

la mesa
table

La piña es una fruta.

la piña

PEE-n'ya

pineapple

Una zanahoria es una verdura y una raíz.

la papa
PA-pa
potato

el huevo
OO'AY-boh
egg

el yogur
ee'oh-GOOR
yogurt

la leche
LAY-chay
milk

la mermelada
mair-meh-LAH-da
jam

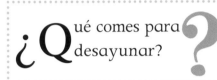

¿**Q**ué comes para desayunar? **?**

Me gusta el pan con miel.

el pan
PAN
bread

la mantequilla
man-tay-KEE-l'ya
butter

la miel
MEE'EL
honey

la pasta
PAS-tah
pasta

el arroz
rice

la carne
KAR-nay
meat

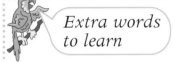

Extra words to learn

el azúcar
ah-soo-kar
sugar

la cebolla
say-BOH-l'yah
onion

la ensalada
en-sa-LAH-da
salad

los espaguetis
ess-pa-GAY-tees
spaghetti

la fruta
FROO-tah
fruit

la galleta
ga-L'YE-tah
cookie

la harina
ah-REE-nah
flour

el pollo
PO-l'yo
chicken

la verdura
bair-DOO-ra
vegetable

Food

A carrot is a vegetable and a root.

De compras
Shopping

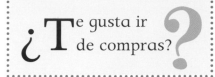

el mercado
mair-KAH-do
market

el precio
price

el dinero
de-NAY-roh
money

la bolsa de la compra
BOL-sah day la KOM-prah
shopping bag

Tengo que comprar comida.

Esperamos en la cola.

el carrito de compras
KA-RREE-toh day KOM-prahs
shopping cart

la cesta
SESS-tah
basket

El primer carrito de compras se inventó hace más de 60 años.

De compras

la camarera
ka-ma-RAY-ra
waitress

el café
ka-FAY
café

pan
huevos
leche
mantequilla
fruta
harina

la lista de la compra
LEES-tah day la KOM-prah
shopping list

el supermercado
soo-pair-mair-KAH-do
supermarket

la panadería
pah-nah-day-REE-ah
bakery

Ella tiene muchas bolsas de compra.

la librería
le-bray-REE-ah
bookstore

la clienta
klee-EN-tay
shopper

Extra words to learn

la caja
KAH-Hah
checkout

la caja registradora
KAH-Hah rreh-Hiss-trah-DOH-rah
cash register

la cuenta
KOO'AYN-tah
bill

el dinero en efectivo
de-NAY-roh en ay'fek-TEE-bo
cash

el precio
PRAY-se'oh
price

el recibo
rray-SE-bo
receipt

la tienda
tee'ayn-da
shop

el vendedor
ben-day-DOR
shopkeeper

Shopping

The first shopping cart was invented more than 60 years ago.

la bebida

beh-BE-da

drink

los sándwiches

SAHND-oo'ich-es

sandwiches

las tarjetas

tar-HAY-tays

cards

las velas

VAY-lahs

candles

el pastel

pahs-TEHL

cake

En la fiesta

At the party

Es divertido jugar con los globos.

Nos gusta bailar con la música.

el reproductor de discos compactos

ray-proh-dook-TOHR day DISS-koss kom-PAK-tohs

CD player

el mago

MAH-go

magician

¿Ves el pastel de cumpleaños?

las decoraciones
day-ko-rah-SE'O-nays
decorations

¡Feliz cumpleaños!

¡Eso es asombroso!

Quiero abrir los regalos.

los regalos de cumpleaños
ray-GAH-los day koom-play-AH-n'yos
birthday presents

¿Ves las tarjetas de felicitación?

los globos
GLOH-bos
balloons

la cámara
KA-mah-rah
camera

las galletas
ga-L'YE-tahs
cookies

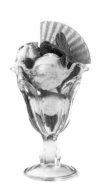

el helado
eh-LAH-do
ice cream

los caramelos
ka-ra-MAY-los
candy

A jugar
Playtime

Extra words to learn

el juego de tablero
HOO'AY-go day tah-BLAY-ro
board game

la pelota
pay-LOH-tah
ball

el robot
rro-BOT
robot

las escondidas
ays-kon-DEE-das
hide-and-seek

el juego
HOO'AY-go
game

el juguete
Hoo-GAY-tay
toy

el libro
LEE-bro
book

la marioneta
mah-re'oh-nay-ta
puppet

la máscara
MAHS-kah-rah
mask

la muñeca
moo-N'YEH-kah
doll

el patinaje
pa-te-NAH-Hay
skating

los dados
DAH-doss
dice

la computadora portátil
kom-poo-tah-DOO-rah pohr-TAH-teel
laptop

Juego con mi tren eléctrico.

el tren
train

el lápiz de color
colored pencil

el dibujo
dee-BOO-ho
drawing

el rompecabezas
rrom-pay-kah-BAY-sas
puzzle

el tren eléctrico
TREN ay-LEK-tree-ko
train set

La primera computadora portátil se fabricó hace más de 20 años.

las cartas
KAHR-tahs
cards

los discos compactos
DISS-kos kom-PAK-tohs
CDs

el reproductor de discos compactos
ray-proh-dook-TOHR day DISS-koss kom-PAK-tohs
CD player

el videojuego
BEE-day-oh-HOO'AY-go
video game

el casco
helmet

el patinaje en línea
pa-te-NAH-Hay en LEE-nee'ah
inline skating

¡Se mueve muy rápido!

la marioneta
puppet

el espactáculo de marionetas
ess-pehk-TAH-koo-lo day mah-re'oh-NAY-ta
puppet show

¡Nos encantan los espectáculos de marionetas!

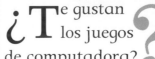

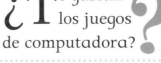

el disfraz
diss-FRAS
costume

el osito
de peluche
teddy bear

¿Te gustan los juegos de computadora?

The first laptop was made more than 20 years ago.

Los transportes

Transportation

el avión
ah-BEE'ON
plane

el transbordador
trans-bor-dah-DOR
ferry

el velero
bay-LAY-ro
sailboat

el taxi
TAK-see
taxi

el camión
ka-ME'ON
truck

Un autobús lleva a la gente de viaje.

la bicicleta
be-se-KLAY-tah
bicycle

el autobús
ah'oo-to-BOOSS
bus

Al rescate

To the rescue

la escalera
ladder

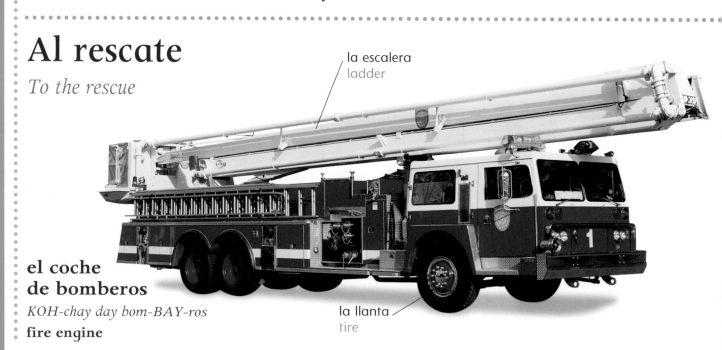

el coche de bomberos
KOH-chay day bom-BAY-ros
fire engine

la llanta
tire

La locomotora más rápida alcanzó 407 millas por hora (655 kph) en 1998.

Los transportes

Un globo aerostático flota en el aire.

la cesta
basket

el globo aerostático
GLO-bo ah-ay-ros-TAH-te-ko
hot air balloon

el tren
TREN
train

el equipaje
luggage

el espejo
mirror

el auto
AH'OO-toh
car

la motocicleta
mo-to-see-KLAY-tah
motorcycle

¿**C**uántas
ruedas hay
en esta página? **?**

el helicóptero de
la policía
*eh-le-KOP-tay-ro day
lah poh-le-SEE-ah*
police helicopter

el coche de policía
ko-chay day poh-le-SEE-ah
police car

la ambulancia
ahm-boo-LAN-se'ah
ambulance

The fastest fire engine reached 407 miles per hour (655 kph) in 1998.

Transportation

Los animales de la jungla

Jungle animals

el ala
wing

la mariposa
mah-re-PO-sah
butterfly

la araña
ah-RA-n'ya
spider

el chimpancé
chem-pahn-SAY
chimpanzee

el gorila
go-REE-la
gorilla

el colibrí
ko-le-BREE
hummingbird

el murciélago
moor-SE'AY-lah-go
bat

la hormiga
or-MEE-gah
ant

la polilla
poh-LEE-l'ya
moth

¿**Q**ué animales pueden volar? **?**

el cocodrilo
ko-ko-DREE-lo
crocodile

La jungla más grande del mundo está en América del Sur.

Los animales de la jungla

el loro
LOH-roh
parrot

Un tucán come comida con el pico.

el ojo
eye

el pico
beak

el tucán
too-KAN
toucan

la garra
claw

la serpiente
sair-PEE'EN'tay
snake

la rana
RRAH-na
frog

la pata
foot

las rayas
stripes

las manchas
spots

el tigre
TEE-gray
tiger

el leopardo
lay-o-PAHR-do
leopard

Jungle animals

The biggest jungle in the world is in South America.

Los animales del mundo *World animals*

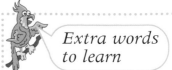

Extra words to learn

el koala
ko-AH-la
koala

el ciervo
SE'AIR-boh
deer

el panda
PAHN-dah
panda

la pata
paw

el león
lay-ON
lion

¡La jirafa tiene un cuello largo!

la jirafa
Hee-RAH-fah
giraffe

el oso polar
O-so poh-LAR
polar bear

el babuino
bah-boo-EE-no
baboon

el caimán
kah-ee-MAN
alligator

el halcón
ahl-KON
hawk

el lobo
LOH-bo
wolf

el murciélago
moor-SE'AY-lah-go
bat

el pelícano
pay-LEE-kah-no
pelican

la tortuga
tohr-TOO-ga
tortoise

el zorro
soh-rro
fox

el pico
beak

la cola
tail

el pingüino
peen-GOO'E-no
penguin

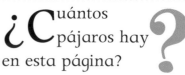

¿**C**uántos pájaros hay en esta página?

¡Una jirafa tiene el mismo número de huesos en el cuello que tú!

el camello
kah-MAY-l'yo
camel

El elefante sostiene comida con su trompa.

las rayas
stripes

la cebra
SAY-bra
zebra

la trompa
trunk

el elefante
ay-lay-FAHN-tay
elephant

el canguro
kan-GOO-ro
kangaroo

la cola
tail

el oso
O-so
bear

la garra
claw

el delfín
del-FEEN
dolphin

la aleta
flipper

el rinoceronte
rree-no-say-RON-tay
rhinoceros

A giraffe has the same number of bones in its neck as you!

el campo
KAM-poh
field

el tractor
TRAK-tor
tractor

el trigo
TREE-go
wheat

los corderos
kor-DAY-rohs
lambs

el perro pastor
PAIR-rro pass-TOR
sheepdog

En la granja
On the farm

El granjero usa el tractor.

la granjera
grahn-HAY-rah
farmer

La vaca come hierba en el campo.

Ana le da leche al cordero.

el trigo
TREE-go
wheat

la cosechadora combinada
koh-say-chah-DO-rah kom-be-NAH-da
combine harvester

la cerca
SAYR-kah
fence

El caballo es café y blanco.

Las vacas bebés se llaman "terneros."

el pato
PAH-to
duck

El pollito está cerca de su madre.

la vaca
BAH-kah
cow

el heno
AY-no
hay

el caballo
kah-BAH-l'yo
horse

el pollo
PO-l'yo
chicken

los patitos
pah-TEE-tos
ducklings

El océano

Ocean

el barco de pesca
BAR-ko day PES-ka
fishing boat

la gaviota
ga-be-OH-ta
seagull

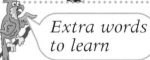

Extra words to learn

el ancla
AN-klah
anchor

el bote de remos
BOH-tay day REH-mos
rowing boat

la boya
BOH-yah
buoy

la langosta
lan-GOSS-ta
lobster

el mar
MAHR
sea

la ola
O-la
wave

el puerto
POO'AIR-to
harbor

la vela
sail

El velero es amarillo y violeta.

el velero
bay-LAY-ro
sailboat

la cuerda
rope

el marinero
mah-ree-NAY-ro
sailor

La ballena nada en el mar.

la ballena
ba-L'YAY-na
whale

la medusa
meh-DOO-sa
jellyfish

El océano

Los océanos cubren casi tres cuartas partes de la superficie de la Tierra.

¿**D**e qué color es el submarino?

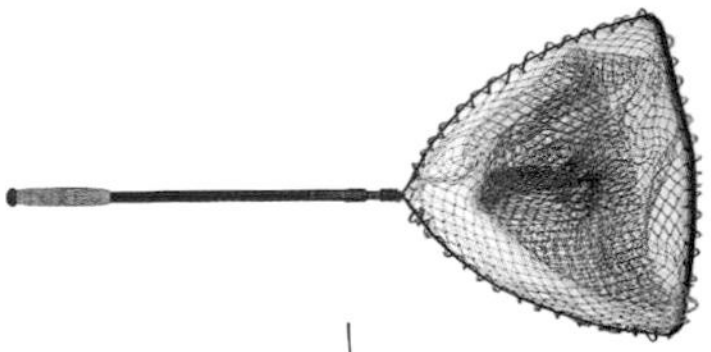

la red
RRED
net

el barco
BAR-ko
ship

el bote salvavidas
BO-tay sal-bah-BEE-das
lifeboat

el faro
FAH-ro
lighthouse

la aleta
fin

el pez
pes
fish

El tiburón tiene muchos dientes.

el tiburón
te-BOO-ron
shark

el alga
AHL-ga
seaweed

el submarino
soob-mah-REE-no
submarine

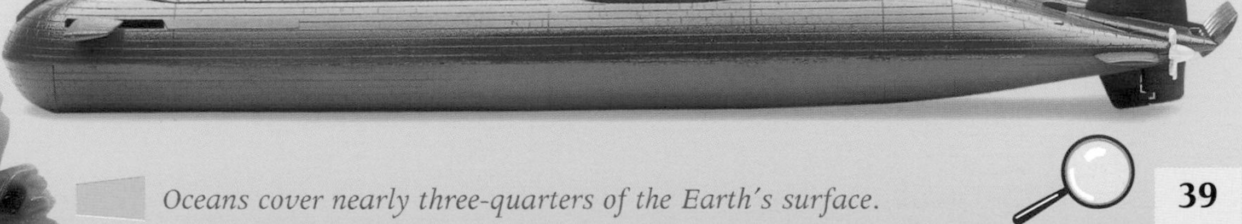

Oceans cover nearly three-quarters of the Earth's surface.

Ocean

39

La naturaleza
Nature

Un nenúfar crece en el agua.

el pico
beak

la planta
PLAHN-ta
plant

la libélula
lee-BEH-loo-lah
dragonfly

el nenúfar
nay-NOO-far
water lily

el pato
PAH-to
duck

Muchos animales viven cerca de estanques.

el cisne
SISS-nay
swan

el sapo
SAH-po
toad

Los sapos normalmente tiene la piel rugosa y las ranas tienen la piel lisa.

el nido
NEE-doh
nest

Los renacuajos nadan en el estanque.

los renacuajos
rray-nah-KOO'AH-Hoh
tadpoles

la antena
antenna

la avispa
ah-BEES-pa
wasp

¿**C**uántos **C**enúfares hay en el estanque **?**

el ala
wing

la mosca
MOSS-ka
fly

el estanque
es-TAN-kay
pond

el búho
BOO-oh
owl

la rana
RRAH-na
frog

Extra words to learn

el agua
ah-GOO'AH
water

el conejo
ko-NAY-ho
rabbit

la garza
GAR-sah
heron

el hábitat
AH-be-taht
habitat

el insecto
in-SEK-to
insect

la mala hierba
MAH-la EE'AIR-ba
weed

la mariposa
mah-re-PO-sah
butterfly

el pájaro
PAH-Hah-ro
bird

Nature

Toads usually have rough skin and frogs have smooth skin.

el cubo
KOO-bo
bucket

la pala
PAH-la
shovel

el cangrejo
kan-GRAY-Ho
crab

la concha
KOHN-cha
shell

los guijarros
ghee-HAH-rros
pebbles

En la playa
At the beach

¡Me encanta nadar en el mar!

¿Te gusta ir a la playa?

Juego bajo mi sombrilla.

la roca
ROH-ka
rock

el protector solar
sunblock

las gaviotas
ga-be-OH-tas
seagulls

Nos encanta jugar con la arena.

Llevo gafas de agua.

la estrella de mar
ess-TRAY-l'ya day MAHR
starfish

el helado
eh-LAH-do
ice cream

el alga
AHL-ga
seaweed

Hacemos un castillo de arena.

las gafas de agua
GAH-fas day AH-goo'ah
goggles

la silla de playa
SEE-l'ya day PLAH-yah
deck chair

la pamela
pa-MAY-la
sunhat

la arena
ah-RAY-na
sand

el castillo de arena
kass-TEE-l'yo day ah-RAY-na
sandcastle

La escuela
School

las tijeras
tee-HAY-ras
scissors

los lápices de colores
LAH-pee-says day ko-LO-rays
colored pencils

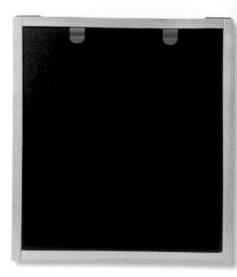

el pizarrón
pe-SAH-rrah
blackboard

la regla
RAY-glah
ruler

la goma
GOH-ma
eraser

el lápiz
LAH-pis
pencil

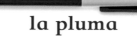

la pluma
PLOO-mah
pen

la libreta
notebook

el escritorio
ess-kre-TO-re'oh
desk

Los niños se sientan en escritorios en la clase.

Extra words to learn

el alfabeto
ahl-fah-BAY-to
alphabet

las ciencias
SEE'EN-see'as
science

el dibujo
dee-BOO-ho
drawing

la escritura
ess-kree-TOO-ra
writing

la lectura
lek-TOO-ra
reading

el maestro
mah-ess-tro
teacher

el salón de clase
sah-LON day KLAH-say
classroom

la silla
SEE-l'yah
chair

¡El lápiz más largo del mundo mide casi 65 pies (20 m)!

¿Ves mi almuerzo en la lonchera?

la lonchera
lohn-CHAY-rah
lunch box

¿**C**uántos **C**libros hay en esta página?

los marcadores
mahr-ka-DO-rays
markers

la libreta
lee-BRAY-tah
notebook

la bolsa de la escuela
school bag

Busca tu país en un globo terráqueo.

el globo terráqueo
GLO-bo tay-RRAH-kay-oh
globe

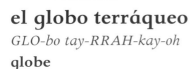

el uniforme escolar
oo-nee-FOHR-may ess-ko-LAR
school uniform

la computadora
kom-poo-tah-DO-rah
computer

los libros
LEE-bros
books

School

The longest pencil in the world is almost 65 feet (20 m) long!

45

Los deportes
Sports

Llevo un casco.

el casco
helmet

la raqueta
rrah-KAY-ta
racket

el esquí
ski

el ciclismo
see-KLEES-moh
cycling

la rueda
wheel

esquiar
ess-ke-AR
skiing

**el patinaje
sobre hielo**
*pa-TE-na-Hay
SO-bray E'AY-lo*
ice skating

la gimnasia
Heem-NAH-se'ah
gymnastics

Jugamos a básquetbol.

Amalia quiere marcar un gol.

la camiseta
T-shirt

los pantalones
cortos
shorts

las zapatillas
deportivas
sneakers

el básquetbol
BAHS-ket-bol
basketball

el golf
GOHLF
golf

el fútbol
foot-bol
soccer

¡Hay unos 28 deportes en los Juegos Olímpicos de verano!

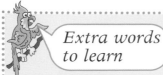

Extra words to learn

el atletismo
aht-lay-tees-moh
athletics

el ejercicio
ay-HAIR-CE-ce'oh
exercise

el hockey
HOH-kay
hockey

el hockey sobre hielo
HOH-kay so-bray E'AY-lo
ice hockey

el judo
JOO-do
judo

el karate
ka-RAH-tay
karate

la natación
na-ta-SE'ON
swimming

¿Te gustan los deportes y hacer ejercicio?

la vela
sail

el chaleco salvavidas
life jacket

tirarse de cabeza
tee-RAR-say day kah-BEH-sah
diving

navegar
na-bay-GAR
sailing

Yo remo.

el remo
oar

el bote
boat

la bola
ball

el guante
glove

remar
rray-MAR
rowing

el bate
bat

el béisbol
BAY-ESS-bol
baseball

la raqueta
racket

el caballo
horse

el rugby
RROOG-be
rugby

correr
ko-RRER
running

montar a caballo
mon-TAR ah kah-BAH-l'yo
horseback riding

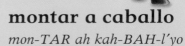

el tenis
tay-niss
tennis

There are about 28 sports in the summer Olympic Games!

Sports

Las mascotas
Pets

Mi perro se llama Miel.

la comida
food

el tazón
bowl

el perrito
pair-RREE-to
puppy

Mi tortuga se mueve muy despacio.

el hámster
HAHMS-tair
hamster

la tortuga
tohr-TOO-ga
tortoise

el collar
collar

el conejillo de indias
ko-nay-Hee-l'yo day IN-de'ahs
guinea pig

el conejo
ko-NAY-ho
rabbit

¿**D**e qué colores es la piel del conejillo de indias?

el gato
GAH-to
cat

el pececito de colores
pay-say-SEE-toh day ko-LO-rehs
goldfish

48   Un gato duerme unas 16 horas al día.

la piel
fur

el gatito
gah-TEE-to
kitten

la lengua
tongue

el perro
PAIR-rroh
dog

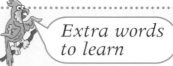

Extra words
to learn

la aleta
ah-LAY-ta
fin

la cola
KOH-la
tail

el collar
koh-L'YAR
collar

la garra
GAH-rrah
claw

la pata
PAH-ta
paw

el pez
pes
fish

la pluma
PLOO-mah
feather

la veterinaria
bay-tair-ree-NAR-re'a
vet

Un loro tiene plumas de colores.

el pico
beak

el loro
LOH-roh
parrot

el pájaro
PAH-Hah-ro
bird

Sam cepilla al caballo.

el bigote
whisker

la cola
tail

el ratón
rah-TON
mouse

el caballo
kah-BAH-l'yo
horse

A cat sleeps about 16 hours a day.

Colores y figuras
Colors and shapes

rojo
RROH-Ho
red

anaranjado
ah-nah-ran-HAH-do
orange

amarillo
ah-mah-REE-l'yo
yellow

verde
BAIR-day
green

azul
ah-SOOL
blue

violeta
be'oh-LAY-ta
purple

rosa
RROH-sa
pink

café
ka-FAY
brown

negro
NAY-gro
black

curvado
curved

recto
straight

¿**C**uál es tu color favorito y tu figura favorita?

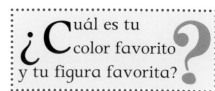

 Todos los colores son una mezcla de rojo, amarillo o azul.

Colores y figuras

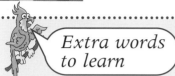
el arcoiris
rainbow

el cuadrado
koo'ah-DRAH-do
square

el círculo
SEER-koo-lo
circle

el triángulo
tree-AHN-goo-lo
triangle

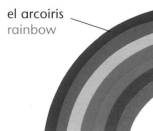

el diamante
de'ah-MAHN-tay
diamond

la estrella
ess-TRAY-l'ya
star

el rectángulo
rrehk-TAN-goo-lo
rectangle

el cubo
KOO-bo
cube

la bola
BO-lah
ball

> ### Extra words to learn
>
> **blanco**
> *BLAHN-ko*
> white
>
> **colorido**
> *ko-lo-RE-do*
> colorful
>
> **el corazón**
> *ko-rah-SON*
> heart
>
> **curvado**
> *koor-BAH-do*
> curved
>
> **el óvalo**
> *OH-bah-lo*
> oval
>
> **recto**
> *RREK-to*
> straight
>
> **redondo**
> *RRAY-don-do*
> round
>
> **el semicírculo**
> *say-me-SEER-koo-lo*
> semicircle

Colors and shapes

All colors are a mixture of red, yellow, or blue.

Los opuestos
Opposites

¡Ábrela bien!

abierto
ah-BE'AIR-toh
open

cerrado
sair-RRAH-do
closed

sucio
soo-se'oh
dirty

rugoso
RROO-go-so
rough

mojado
mo-HAH-do
wet

seco
SAY-ko
dry

limpio
LEEM-pe'oh
clean

liso
LEE-so
smooth

Extra words to learn

lento
LEN-to
slow

ligero
lee-HAY-ro
light

lleno
L'YEH-no
full

nuevo
NOO'AY-bo
new

pesado
pay-SAH-do
heavy

rápido
RRAH-pe-do
fast

vacío
bah-SE'oh
empty

viejo
BE'AY-Ho
old

  ¡La mayoría de las calabazas son anaranjadas, pero también se pueden cultivar blancas y azules!

¿**T**e gustan las bebidas calientes o frías?

Una calabaza se hace gorda en el otoño.

gordo
GOHR-do
fat

frío
FREE-oh
cold

caliente
ka-LE'AYN-tay
hot

Esta verdura es muy delgada.

delgado
dell-GAH-do
thin

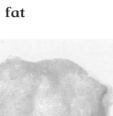

blando
BLAHN-do
soft

duro
DOO-ro
hard

Un girasol se hace alto.

Esta flor es baja.

bajo
BAH-Ho
short

alto
AHL-to
tall

pequeño
pay-KAY-n'yo
small

grande
GRAHN-day
big

Opposites

Most pumpkins are orange, but you can grow white and blue ones!

el muñeco de nieve
moo-N'YEH-ko day NEE'AY-bay
snowman

la nieve
NEE'AY-bay
snow

el gorro de lana
GO-rroh day LAH-na
wool hat

El tiempo
Weather

el otoño
oh-TO-n'yo
fall

los copos de nieve
KOH-pos day NEE'AY-bay
snowflakes

Me gusta hacer un muñeco de nieve.

Llevo un gorro, una bufanda y guantes.

Hoy hace mucho viento.

el paraguas
pair-RAH-goo'ahs
umbrella

la primavera
pree-ma-BAY-ra
spring

el verano
bay-RAH-no
summer

el sol
SOHL
sun

Hace calor al sol.

la lluvia
LYU-be'ah
rain

la nube
NOO-bay
cloud

el arcoiris
ar-ko-EE-ris
rainbow

las gafas de sol
GAH-fas day SOHL
sunglasses

la gorra
GO-rrah
cap

A
B
C
D
E
F
G
H
I
J
K
L
M
N
O
P
Q
R
S
T
U
V
W
X
Y
Z

English A–Z

In this section, English words are in alphabetical order, followed by the Spanish translation. There is information after each English word to show you what type of word it is. This will help you to make sentences. In Spanish, nouns (naming words) are either masculine (m) or feminine (f). If the Spanish word has *el* before it, it is masculine; if it has *la*, it is feminine.

(**n**) = noun (a naming word). Either masculine or feminine. Feminine nouns usually have an "a" at the end.

(**adj**) = adjective (a describing word). These words can change depending on whether the noun they are describing is masculine or feminine.

(**adv**) = adverb (a word that gives more information about a verb, an adjective, or another adverb)

(**conj**) = conjunction (a joining word, e.g., and)

(**prep**) = preposition (e.g., about)

(**pron**) = pronoun (e.g., he, she, it)

(**article**) = (e.g., a, an, the)

(**sing**) = singular (one thing)   (**plu**) = plural (lots of things)

apple
la manzana

a (article)
un (m) una (f)
OON/OON-a

about (adv)
sobre/acerca de
SO-bray/ah-SAIR-kah day

above (prep)
sobre
SO-bray

accident (n)
el accidente
ahk-se-DEN-tay

across (prep)
a través de
ah trah-BESS day

activity (n)
la actividad
ahk-te-bi-DAHD

address (n)
la dirección
dee-rek-se'ON

adult (adj)
adulto (m)
ah-DOOL-toh

adventure (n)
la aventura
a-ben-TOO-rah

after (prep)
después de/tras
dess-poo'ESS/TRAHS

afternoon (n)
la tarde
TAR-day

again (adv)
otra vez
O-tra BES

de nuevo
day NOO'AY-boh

age (n)
la edad
ay-DAHD

air (n)
el aire
AH'E-ray

airplane (n)
el avión
ah-BEE'ON

airport (n)
el aeropuerto
ah-ay-ro-poo'AIR-to

alarm clock (n)
el despertador
dess-pair-tah-DOR

all (adj)
todo (m)
TO-do

alligator (n)
el caimán
kah-ee-MAN

almost (adv)
casi
KAH-see

alone (adj)
solo (m)
SOH-lo

alphabet (n)
el alfabeto
ahl-fah-BAY-to

el abecedario
ah-bay-say-DHA-re'oh

already (adv)
ya
YAH

also (adv)
también
tahm-BE'EN

always (adv)
siempre
SE'EM-pray

amazing (adj)
asombroso (m)
ah-som-BROH-so

ambulance (n)
la ambulancia
ahm-boo-LAN-se'ah

an (article)
un (m) una (f)
OON/OON-a

anchor (n)
el ancla
AN-klah

and (conj)
y (except before i/hi)
e

e (before i/hi)
eh

airplane
el avión

angry (adj)
enfadado (m)
en-fah-DAH-do

animal (n)
el animal
ah-ne-MAHL

ankle (n)
el tobillo
to-BEE-l'yo

answer (n)
la respuesta
rres-poo'EES-tah

ant (n)
la hormiga
or-MEE-gah

antenna (n)
la antena
ahn-TAY-nah

any (adj)
cualquiera
koo-ahl-ke-AY-ra

anyone/anything (pron)
cualquiera
koo-ahl-ke-AY-ra

apart (adv)
aparte
ah-PAR-tay

apartment (n)
el apartamento
ah-par-tah-MEN-to

appearance (n)
la apariencia
ah-pah-RE'En-sia

apple (n)
la manzana
mahn-SAH-nah

apron (n)
el delantal
day-lahn-TAHL

arch (n)
el arco
AR-ko

area (n)
el área
AH-ray'ah

arm (n)
el brazo
BRAH-so

armchair (n)
el sillón
se-L'YON

army (n)
el ejército
eh-HAIR-se-to

around (prep)
alrededor
ahl-ray-day-DOR

armchair
sillón

arrival (n)
la llegada
l'yay-GAH-da

arrow (n)
la flecha
FLAY-chah

art (n)
el arte
AR-tay

artist (n)
el/la artista
ar-TEES-tah

assistant (n)
el/la asistente
ah-siss-TEN-tah

astronaut (n)
el/la astronauta
ahs-tro-NAH'OO-tah

astronomer (n)
el astrónomo
ahs-TRO-noh-mo

la astrónoma
ahs-TRO-noh-ma

athletics (n)
el atletismo
aht-lay-tees-moh

atlas (n)
el atlas
AHT-lahs

attic (n)
el ático
AH-tee-ko

aunt (n)
la tía
TEE-ah

avocado (n)
el aguacate
ah-goo'ah-KAH-tay

astronaut
la astronauta

avocado
el aguacate

A B C D E F G H I J K L M N O P Q R S T U V W X Y Z

B

balloon
el globo

baboon (n)
el **babuino**
bah-boo-EE-no

baby (n)
el **bebé**
beh-BEH

back (adj)
de **atrás**
day ah-TRAHS

back (body) (n)
la **espalda**
ess-PAHL-dah

backpack (n)
la **mochila**
mo-CHEE-lah

backward (adv)
hacia atrás
A-se'ah ah-TRAHS

bad (adj)
malo (m)
MAH-lo

badge (n)
la **insignia**
in-SIG-ne'ah

badminton (n)
el **bádminton**
BAHD-meen-ton

bag (n)
la **bolsa**
BOL-sah

bakery (n)
la **panadería**
pah-nah-day-REE-ah

balcony (n)
el **balcón**
bahl-KON

ball (n)
la **pelota**
pay-LOH-tah

la **bola**
BO-lah

ballet dancer (n)
el **bailarín**
bah'e-lah-REEN

la **bailarina**
bah'e-lah-REE-nah

balloon (n)
el **globo**
GLOH-bo

banana (n)
el **plátano**
PLAH-tah-no

band (n)
la **banda**
BAHN-dah

bank (money) (n)
el **banco**
BAHN-ko

bank (river) (n)
la **orilla**
o-REE-l'ya

barbecue (n)
la **barbacoa**
bar-bah-KO-ah

barn (n)
el **granero**
grah-NAY-ro

baseball (n)
el **béisbol**
BAY'ESS-bol

basement (n)
el **sótano**
SO-tah -no

basket (n)
la **cesta**
SESS-tah

basketball (n)
el **básquetbol**
BAHS-ket-bol

bat (animal) (n)
el **murciélago**
moor-SE'AY-lah-go

bat (sports) (n)
el **bate**
BAH-teh

bath (n)
el **baño**
BAHN-n'yo

bathroom (n)
el **(cuarto de) baño**
(KOO'AR-toh de)
BAH-n'yo

bat
el murciélago

battery (n)
la **pila**
PEE-lah

battle (n)
la **batalla**
bah-TAH-l'yah

beach (n)
la **playa**
PLAH-yah

bead (n)
la **cuenta**
KOO'EN-tah

beak (n)
el **pico**
PEE-koh

beans (n)
los **frijoles**
free-HO-lays

bear (n)
el **oso**
O-so

beard (n)
la **barba**
BAHR-bah

beautiful (adj)
bonito (m)
boh-NEE-toh

beauty (n)
la **belleza**
bay-L'YE-sah

because (conj)
porque
POHR-kay

bear
el oso

A B C D E F G H I J K L M N O P Q R S T U V W X Y Z

bed (n)
la **cama**
KAH-mah

bedroom (n)
el **dormitorio**
dohr-me-TOH-re'oh

bee (n)
la **abeja**
ah-BAY-Hah

beetle (n)
el **escarabajo**
es-kah-rah-BA-Hoh

before (prep)
antes
AHN-tess

behind (prep)
detrás
day- TRAHS

bell (n)
la **campana**
kahm-PAH-nah

below (prep)
abajo
ah-BAH-Ho

debajo
day-BAH-Ho

belt (n)
el **cinturón**
sin-too-RON

bench (n)
el **banco**
BAHN-ko

bicycle
la bicicleta

saddle
el sillín

tire
la llanta

pedal
el pedal

wheel
la rueda

binoculars
los binoculares

best (pron)
el/la **mejor**
MAY-Hor

better (adj)
mejor
MAY-Hor

between (prep)
entre
EN-tray

bicycle (n)
la **bicicleta**
be-se-KLAY-tah

big (adj)
gran (before noun)
GRAHN

grande (after noun)
GRAHN-day

bill (n)
la **factura**
fak-TOO-rah

la **cuenta**
KOO'AYN-tah

billion
billón
bee-l'yon

binoculars (n)
los **binoculares**
be-noh-koo-LAH-rehs

bird (n)
el **pájaro**
PAH-Hah-ro

birthday (n)
el **cumpleaños**
koom-play-AH-n'yos

birthday present (n)
el **regalo de cumpleaños**
ray-GAH-lo day
koom-play-AH-n'yos

black (adj)
negro (m)
NAY-gro

blackboard (n)
el **pizarrón**
pe-SAH-rrah

blanket (n)
la **manta**
MAHN-tah

blonde (adj)
rubio (m)
ROO-bee'o

blood (n)
la **sangre**
SAHN-gray

blouse (n)
la **blusa**
BLOO-sah

blue (adj)
azul
ah-SOOL

board (n)
el **tablero**
tah-BLAY-ro

board game (n)
el **juego de tablero**
HOO'AY-go day
tah-BLAY-ro

A
B
C
D
E
F
G
H
I
J
K
L
M
N
O
P
Q
R
S
T
U
V
W
X
Y
Z

boat (n)
el bote
BO-tay

body (n)
el cuerpo
KOO'AIR-po

bone (n)
el hueso
OO'AY-so

book (n)
el libro
LEE-bro

bookstore (n)
la librería
le-bray-REE-ah

boot (n)
la bota
bo-tah

boring (adj)
aburrido (m)
ah-boo-RREE-doh

bottle (n)
la botella
bo-TAY-l'yah

bottom (n)
el fondo
FON-do

bowl (n)
el tazón
tah-SON

box (n)
la caja
KAH-Ha

boy (n)
el niño
NEE-n'yoh

el chico
CHEE-ko

boyfriend (n)
el novio
NO-be'oh

bracelet (n)
la pulsera
pool-SAY-rah

brain (n)
el cerebro
say-RAY-bro

branch (n)
la rama
RRAH-mah

brave (adj)
valiente
bah-LE'EN-tay

bread (n)
el pan
PAN

break (n)
el recreo
ray-CRAY-oh

breakfast (n)
el desayuno
deh-sah-YOO-no

breeze (n)
la brisa
BREE-sa

bubbles
las burbujas

butterfly
la mariposa

bridge (n)
el puente
POO'EN-tay

bright (adj)
brillante
bree-L'YAN-tay

broken (adj)
roto (m)
RROH-toh

broom (n)
la escoba
ess-KO-bah

brother (n)
el hermano
air-MAH-noh

brown (adj)
café
ka-FAY

bubble (n)
la burbuja
boor-BOO-Hah

bucket (n)
el cubo
KOO-bo

building (n)
el edificio
eh-dee-FEE-se'oh

bulb (plant) (n)
el bulbo
BOOL-boh

buoy (n)
la boya
BOH-yah

bus (n)
el autobús
ah'oo-to-BOOSS

bus stop (n)
la parada del
autobús
*pah-RAH-dah del
ah'oo-to-BOOSS*

bush (n)
el arbusto
ar-BOOSS-to

business (n)
el negocio
nay-GO-se'oh

busy (adj)
ocupado (m)
oh-koo-PAH-do

but (conj)
pero
PAY-roh

butter (n)
la mantequilla
man-tay-KEE-l'ya

butterfly (n)
la mariposa
mah-re-PO-sah

button (n)
el botón
bo-TON

C

cake
el pastel

cabbage (n)
la col
KOL

café (n)
el café
ka-FAY

cage (n)
la jaula
HA'OO-lah

cake (n)
el pastel
pahs-TEHL

calculator (n)
la calculadora
kahl-koo-lah-DO-rah

calendar (n)
el calendario
kah-len-DAH-ree'oh

calf (animal) (n)
el ternero
tair-NAY-ro

calm (adj)
calmado (m)
kahl-MAH-do

camel (n)
el camello
kah-MAY-l'yo

camera (n)
la cámara
KA-mah-rah

camping (n)
la acampada
ah-kahm-PAH-da

can (n)
la lata
LAH-ta

candle (n)
la vela
VAY-lah

candy (n)
el caramelo
ka-ra-MAY-lo

canoe (n)
la canoa
ka-NO-ah

cap (n)
la gorra
GO-rrah

capital (n)
la capital
ka-pe-TAHL

car (n)
el auto
AH'OO-toh

card (greeting) (n)
la tarjeta
tar-HAY-tah

card (playing) (n)
la carta
KAHR-tah

cardboard (n)
el cartón
kar-TON

careful (adj)
cuidadoso (m)
koo'e-dah-DO-so

carpet (n)
la alfombra
ahl-FOM-brah

carrot (n)
la zanahoria
sah-nah-O-re'ah

cart (n)
el carro
KAR-rro

cash (n)
el dinero en
efectivo
de-NAY-roh en
ay-fek-TEE-bo

cash register (n)
la caja registradora
KAH-Hah rreh-Hiss-
trah-DOH-rah

cassette (n)
la cinta
SEEN-tah

cat (n)
el gato
GAH-to

caterpillar (n)
la oruga
o-ROO-gah

cave (n)
la cueva
KOO'AY-ba

CD (n)
el disco compacto
DISS-ko kom-PAK-toh

CD player (n)
el reproductor de
discos compactos
ray-proh-dook-TOHR
day DISS-koss
kom-PAK-tohs

ceiling (n)
el techo
TAY-cho

cellular phone (n)
el teléfono celular
tay-LAY-fo-no cel-loo-LAR

center (n)
el centro
SEN-troh

cereal (n)
el cereal
say-ray-AHL

certain (adj)
seguro (m)
say-GOO-ro

chain (n)
la cadena
kah-DAY-nah

chair (n)
la silla
SEE-l'yah

challenge (n)
el reto
RAY-toh

window
la ventana

door
la puerta

car
el auto

A B C D E F G H I J K L M N O P Q R S T U V W X Y Z

C

change (n)
el **cambio**
KAM-be'oh

cheap (adj)
barato (m)
bah-RAH-to

checkout (n)
la **caja**
KAH-Hah

cheese (n)
el **queso**
KAY-so

chef (n)
el/la **chef**
CHEF

chess (n)
el **ajedrez**
ay-Hay-DRES

chest (n)
el **baúl**
bah-OOL

chest of drawers (n)
la **cómoda**
KO-mo-dah

chewing gum (n)
el **chicle**
CHEE-clay

chick (n)
el **pollito**
po-L'YEE-to
el **pajarito**
pah-Ha-REE-to

chicken (n)
el **pollo**
PO-l'yo

child (n)
el **niño**
NEE-n'yo
la **niña**
NEE-n'ya

children (n)
los **niños**
NEE-n'yos
las **niñas**
NEE-n'yas

chimney (n)
la **chimenea**
che-may-NAY-ah

chimpanzee (n)
el **chimpancé**
chem-pahn-SAY

chin (n)
la **barbilla**
bar-BEE-l'ya

chocolate (n)
el **chocolate**
cho-ko-LAH-tay

cinema (n)
el **cine**
SEE-nay

circle (n)
el **círculo**
SEER-koo-lo

circus (n)
el **circo**
SEER-ko

city (n)
la **ciudad**
se'oo-DAHD

classroom (n)
el **salón de clase**
sah-LON day KLAH-say

claw (n)
la **garra**
GAH-rrah

clean (adj)
limpio (m)
LEEM-pe'oh

clear (adj)
claro (m)
KLAH-ro

clever (adj)
listo (m)
LEES-to

cliff (n)
el **acantilado**
ah-kahn-te-LAH-do

cloak (n)
la **capa**
KAH-pah

clock (n)
el **reloj**
rray-LOH

close (adj)
cercano (m)
sair-KAH-no

closed (adj)
cerrado (m)
sair-RRAH-do

cloth (n)
la **tela**
TAY-lah

clothes (n)
la **ropa**
RROH-pah

cloud (n)
la **nube**
NOO-bay

cloudy (adj)
nublado (m)
noo-BLAH-do

clown (n)
el **payaso**
pah-YAH-so
la **payasa**
pah-YAH-sa

coach (sports) (n)
el **entrenador**
en-tray-nah-DOR
la **entrenadora**
en-tray-nah-DO-rah

coast (n)
la **costa**
KOS-tah

coat (n)
el **abrigo**
ah-BREE-go

coat hanger (n)
la **percha**
PER-chah

coconut (n)
el **coco**
KO-ko

coffee (n)
el **café**
kah-FAY

coin (n)
la **moneda**
moh-NAY-dah

cold (adj)
frío (m)
FREE-oh

collar (n)
el **collar**
koh-L'YAR

college (n)
la **universidad**
oo-ne-bair-se-DAHD

computer
la computadora

hard drive
el disco duro

keyboard
el teclado

screen
la pantalla

mouse pad
la alfombrilla
del ratón

mouse
el ratón

compass
la brújula

color (n)
el color
ko-LOR

colored pencil (n)
el lápiz de color
LAH-pis day ko-LOR

colorful (adj)
colorido (m)
ko-lo-RE-do

comb (n)
el peine
PAY'EH-neh

combine harvester (n)
la cosechadora combinada
koh-say-chah-DO-rah
kom-be-NAH-da

comfortable (adj)
cómodo (m)
KO-mo-doh

comforter (n)
el edredón
ay-dray-DON

comic (n)
la historieta
iss-TO-re-ah

crab
el cangrejo

compass (n)
la brújula
BROO-Hoo-lah

computer (n)
la computadora
kom-poo-tah-DOO-rah

concert (n)
el concierto
kon-SE'AYR-toh

contest (n)
el concurso
kon-KOOR-so

continent (n)
el continente
kon-te-NEN-tay

controls (n)
los mandos
MAN-doss

cookie (n)
la galleta
ga-L'YE-tah

cool (adj)
fresco (m)
FRESS-ko

corner (n)
la esquina
ess-KEE-nah

correct (adj)
correcto (m)
ko-RREHK-to

costume (n)
el disfraz
diss-FRAS

cotton (n)
el algodón
ahl-go-DON

cough (n)
la tos
TOSS

country (n)
el país
pah-ISS

countryside (n)
el campo
KAHM-po

cousin (n)
el primo
PREE-mo

la prima
PREE-ma

cow (n)
la vaca
BAH-kah

cowboy (n)
el vaquero
bah-KAY-ro

cowgirl (n)
la vaquera
bah-KAY-rah

crab (n)
el cangrejo
kan-GRAY-Ho

crane (n)
la grúa
GROO-ah

crayon (n)
el creyón
kray-YON

cream (n)
la crema
KRAY-mah

creature (n)
la criatura
kre-ah-TOO-rah

crew (n)
la tripulación
tre-poo-lah-SE'ON

crocodile (n)
el cocodrilo
ko-ko-DREE-lo

crop (n)
la cosecha
ko-SAY-chah

crossing (n)
el cruce
KROO-say

crowded (adj)
lleno de gente (m)
L'YE-no day HEN-tay

crown (n)
la corona
ko-RO-nah

cube (n)
el cubo
KOO-bo

cup (n)
la taza
TAH-sa

cupboard (n)
la alacena
ah-lah-SAY-nah

curious (adj)
curioso (m)
koo-RE'OH-so

curly (adj)
rizado (m)
rree-SAH-do

curtain (n)
la cortina
kor-TEE-nah

curved (adj)
curvado (m)
koor-BAH-do

cushion (n)
el cojín
ko-HEN

customer (n)
el cliente
klee-AYN-tay

la clienta
klee-AYN-tah

cycling (n)
el ciclismo
see-KLEES-moh

crown
la corona

A
B
C
D
E
F
G
H
I
J
K
L
M
N
O
P
Q
R
S
T
U
V
W
X
Y
Z

A
B
C
D
E
F
G
H
I
J
K
L
M
N
O
P
Q
R
S
T
U
V
W
X
Y
Z

D

daisy
la margarita

dad (n)
el papá
pah-PAH

daisy (n)
la margarita
mar-gah-REE-tah

dam (n)
la presa
PREH-sah

dancer (n)
el bailarín
bah'e-lah-REEN

la bailarina
bah'e-lah-REE-nah

dandelion (n)
el diente de león
DE'AYN-tay day lay-ON

danger (n)
el peligro
peh-LEE-gro

dangerous (adj)
peligroso (m)
peh-lee-GRO-so

dark (adj)
oscuro (m)
ohs-KOO-roh

date (n)
la cita
SEE-ta

daughter (n)
la hija
EE-Hah

day (n)
el día
DEE-a

dead (adj)
muerto (m)
MOO'AIR-toh

deaf (adj)
sordo (m)
SOR-doh

dear (special) (adj)
querido (m)
kay-RE-do

deck (n)
la cubierta
koo-BE'AIR-tah

deck chair (n)
la silla de playa
SEE-l'ya day PLAH-yah

decoration (n)
la decoración
day-ko-rah-SE'ON

deep (adj)
profundo (m)
proh-FOON-do

deer (n)
el ciervo
SE'AIR-boh

delicious (adj)
delicioso (m)
deh-lee-SE'OH-so

dentist (n)
el/la dentista
dehn-TISS-tah

desert (n)
el desierto
deh-SE'AIR-toh

desk (n)
el escritorio
ess-kre-TO-re'oh

dessert (n)
el postre
POS-tray

diagram (n)
el diagrama
de-ah-GRA-mah

diamond (n)
el diamante
de'ah-MAHN-tay

dice (n)
los dados
DAH-doss

dictionary (n)
el diccionario
deek-se'oh-NAH-re'oh

different (adj)
diferente
de-fay-REN-tay

difficult (adj)
difícil
de-FEE-cil

digital (adj)
digital
de-He-TAHL

dining room (n)
el comedor
koh-may-DOHR

dinner (n)
la cena
SAY-nah

dinosaur (n)
el dinosaurio
dee-noh-SAH'OO-re'oh

direction (n)
la dirección
dee-rek-SE'ON

directly (adv)
directamente
dee-REK-tah-MEN-tay

dirty (adj)
sucio (m)
SOO-se'oh

disabled (adj)
minusválido (m)
mee-noos-BAH-le-doh

disco (n)
la disco
DISS-ko

discovery (n)
el descubrimiento
des-koo-bree-ME'AYN-toh

dish towel (n)
el paño de cocina
PAH-n'yo day
ko-SEE-na

distance (n)
la distancia
diss-TAHN-se'ah

divorced (adj)
divorciado (m)
dee-bor-SE'AH-do

doctor (n)
el doctor
dok-TOHR

la doctora
dok-TO-rah

dog (n)
el perro
PAIR-rroh

doll (n)
la muñeca
moo-N'YEH-kah

dolphin (n)
el delfín
del-FEEN

dome (n)
la cúpula
KOO-poo-lah

door (n)
la puerta
POO'AIR-tah

downstairs (n)
el piso de abajo
PE-soh day a-BA-Hoh

dragon (n)
el dragón
drah-GON

dragonfly (n)
la libélula
lee-BEH-loo-lah

drawer (n)
el cajón
kah-HON

drawing (n)
el **dibujo**
dee-BOO-Ho

dream (n)
el **sueño**
SOO'AY-n'yo

dress (n)
el **vestido**
behs-TE-do

drink (n)
la **bebida**
beh-BE-da

drinking straw (n)
la **pajita**
pah-HEE-tah

drop (n)
la **gota**
GO-tah

drum (n)
el **tambor**
tam-BOHR

drum kit (n)
la **batería**
bah-tay-REE-ah

dry (adj)
seco **(m)**
SAY-ko

duck (n)
el **pato**
PAH-to

duckling (n)
el **patito**
pah-TEE-to

during (prep)
durante
doo-RAHN-tay

dust (n)
el **polvo**
POHL-boh

DVD player (n)
el **reproductor de DVD**
rray-pro-dook-TOHR day day-bay-DEH

duck
el pato

E

egg
el huevo

each (adj)
cada
KAH-dah

eagle (n)
el **águila**
AH-ghee-lah

ear (n)
la **oreja**
oh-RAY-Hah

el **oído**
oh-EE-do

earache (n)
el **dolor de oído**
doh-LOHR day oh-EE-do

early (adv)
temprano
tem-PRAH-no

earring (n)
el **arete**
ah-RAY-tay

Earth (planet) (n)
la **Tierra**
TE'AY-rrah

earthworm (n)
el **gusano**
goo-SAH-no

east (n)
el **este**
ESS-tay

easy (adj)
fácil
FAH-sil

echo (n)
el **eco**
AY-koh

edge (n)
el **filo**
FEE-loh

effect (n)
el **efecto**
ay-fek-to

egg (n)
el **huevo**
OO'AY-boh

elbow (n)
el **codo**
KOH-do

electrical (adj)
eléctrico (m)
ay-LEK-tree-ko

elephant (n)
el **elefante**
ay-lay-FAHN-tay

elevator (n)
el **ascensor**
ass-sayn-SOR

email (n)
el **correo electrónico**
ko-RRAY-oh ay-lek-TROH-ne-ko

email address (n)
la **dirección de correo electrónico**
dee-rek-se-ON day ko-RRAY-oh ay-lek-TROH-ne-ko

emergency (n)
la **emergencia**
ay-mehr-HEN-se'ah

empty (adj)
vacío (m)
bah-SE-oh

A B C **D** **E** F G H I J K L M N O P Q R S T U V W X Y Z

E

encyclopedia (n)
la **enciclopedia**
en-se-kloh-PEH-de'ah

end (n)
el **fin**
FEEN

English (n)
el **inglés**
enn-GLAYS

enough (adj)
suficiente
soo-fee-SE'AYN-teh

enthusiastic (adj)
entusiasta
en-too-SE'AHSS-tah

entrance (n)
la **entrada**
en-TRAH-da

envelope (n)
el **sobre**
SOH-bray

environment (n)
el **medio ambiente**
MEH-de'oh
am-BE'AYN-tay

equal (adj)
igual
ee-GOO'AHL

equator (n)
el **ecuador**
ay-koo'ah-DOHR

equipment (n)
el **equipo**
ay-KEE-poh

eraser (n)
la **goma**
GOH-ma

stamp
el sello

Museo de Arte Moderno
Avenida de San Juan, 350
Buenos Aires
ARGENTINA

envelope
el sobre

address
la dirección

even (adv)
hasta
ASS-tah

evening (n)
la **tarde**
TAHR-day

event (n)
el **evento**
ay-BEN-to

every (adj)
cada
KAH-dah

everybody (pron)
todo el mundo
TOH-doh el MOON-doh

everything (pron)
todo
TOH-doh

everywhere (adv)
por todos lados
pohr TOH-doss LAH-doss

exam (n)
el **examen**
ek-SAH-men

excellent (adj)
excelente
ek-say-LAYN-te

excited (adj)
emocionado (m)
eh-mo-ce'oh-NAH-do

exercise (n)
el **ejercicio**
ay-Hair-CE-ce'oh

exit (n)
la **salida**
sa-LEE-da

expedition (n)
la **expedición**
eks-pay-de-CE'ON

expensive (adj)
caro (m)
KAH-roh

experiment (n)
el **experimento**
eks-pay-re-MEN-to

expert (n)
el **experto**
eks-PAIR-to

explorer (n)
el **explorador**
eks-ploh-rah-DOR

explosion (n)
la **explosión**
eks-plo-SE'ON

extinct (adj)
extinto (m)
eks-TEEN-to

extra (adj)
adicional
a-dee-se'oh-NAHL

extremely (adv)
extremadamente
eks-tray-MAH-dah-MEN-tay

eye (n)
el **ojo**
OH-Hoh

eyebrow (n)
la **ceja**
SAY-Hah

eyelash (n)
la **pestaña**
pays-TAH-n'ya

arm
el brazo

exercise
el ejercicio

leg
la pierna

hand
la mano

foot
el pie

F

fashion
la moda

fabulous (adj)
fabuloso (m)
fah-boo-LO-so

face (n)
la cara
KAH-ra

fact (n)
el hecho
AY-cho

factory (n)
la fábrica
FAH-bre-kah

faint (pale) (adj)
pálido (m)
PAH-le-doh

fair (n)
la feria
FAY-re'ah

fall (season) (n)
el otoño
oh-TO-n'yo

false (adj)
falso (m)
FAHL-so

family (n)
la familia
fah-ME-le'ah

famous (adj)
famoso (m)
fah-MOH-so

fantastic (adj)
fantástico (m)
fan-TAHS-te-ko

far (adv)
lejos
LAY-Hos

farm (n)
la granja
GRAHN-Ha

farmer (n)
el granjero
grahn-HAY-ro
la granjera
grahn-HAY-rah

fashion (n)
la moda
MOH-da

fashionable (adj)
de moda
day MOH-da

fast (adv)
rápido (m)
RRAH-pe-do

fat (adj)
gordo (m)
GOHR-do

father (n)
el padre
PAH-dray

faucet (n)
el grifo
GREE-fo

favorite (adj)
favorito (m)
fa-boh-REE-to

feather (n)
la pluma
PLOO-mah

felt (n)
el fieltro
FE'AYL-troh

female (n)
la hembra
EM-brah

fence (n)
la cerca
SAYR-kah

fern (n)
el helecho
ay-LAY-cho

ferry (n)
el transbordador
trans-bor-dah-DOR

festival (n)
el festival
fess-te-VAHL

field (n)
el campo
KAM-poh

fin (n)
la aleta
ah-LAY-ta

fine (adv)
bien
BE'EN

finger (n)
el dedo
DAY-doh

fire (n)
el fuego
FOO'AY-goh

fire engine (n)
el coche de
bomberos
*KOH-chay day
bom-BAY-ros*

firefighter (n)
el bombero
bom-BAY-ro
la bombera
bom-BAY-rah

first (adv)
primero
pre-MAY-ro
en primer lugar
en pre-MAYR loo-GAR

first aid (n)
los primeros
auxilios
*pre-MAY-ros
ah'ook-SE-le'ohs*

fish (n)
el pez
pes

fishing (n)
pescar
pes-KAR

fishing boat (n)
el barco de pesca
BAR-ko day PES-ka

eye
el ojo

fin
la aleta

fish
el pez

A B C D E **F** G H I J K L M N O P Q R S T U V W X Y Z

67

F

fishing line (n)
el **hilo de pescar**
EE-loh day pes-KAR

fist (n)
el **puño**
POO-n'yo

fit (adj)
en forma
en FOHR-ma

flag (n)
la **bandera**
ban-DAY-ra

flap (n)
la **solapa**
so-LAH-pah

flat (adj)
plano (m)
PLAH-no

fleece (clothing) (n)
el **forro polar**
FOR-rro po-LAR

flipper (n)
la **aleta**
ah-LAY-ta

flood (n)
la **inundación**
ee-noon-dah-se'on

floor (n)
el **suelo**
SOO'EH-lo

floor (building) (n)
el **piso**
PEE-so

flour (n)
la **harina**
ah-REE-nah

flower (n)
la **flor**
FLOR

flute (n)
la **flauta**
FLAH'OO-ta

fly (n)
la **mosca**
MOSS-ka

fog (n)
la **niebla**
NEE'EH-blah

food (n)
la **comida**
ko-ME-da

foot (n)
el **pie**
PEE'EH

football (game) (n)
el **fútbol americano**
FOOT-bol
ah-mehr-I-CAHN-oh

foreign (adj)
extranjero (m)
eks-tran-HAY-ro

forest (n)
el **bosque**
BOSS-kay

fork (n)
el **tenedor**
tay-nay-DOR

forward (adv)
adelante
ah-day-LAHN-tay

fossil (n)
el **fósil**
FO-sil

fox (n)
el **zorro**
soh-rro

frame (n)
el **marco**
MAR-ko

free time (n)
el **tiempo libre**
TEE'EM-po LE-bray

freedom (n)
la **libertad**
le-bair-TAHD

freezer (n)
el **congelador**
kon-Hay-la-DOR

French (n)
el **francés**
fran-SEHS

French fries (n)
las **papas fritas**
PAH-pahs FREE-tas

fresh (adj)
fresco (m)
FRAYS-ko

fridge (n)
el **refrigerador**
reh-free-Hay-ra-DOR

friend (n)
el **amigo**
ah-MEE-goh
la **amiga**
ah-MEE-gah

friendly (adj)
amigable
ah-mee-GAH-blay

frightened (adj)
asustado (m)
ah-soos-TA-do

frog (n)
la **rana**
RRAH-na

from (prep)
de
DAY

front door (n)
la **puerta principal**
POO'ER-tah preen-se-PAL

fruit (n)
la **fruta**
FROO-tah

frying pan (n)
la **sartén**
sar-TAYN

full (adj)
lleno (m)
L'YEH-no

fun (n)
divertido (m)
de-vair-TEE-do

fur (n)
la **piel**
PEE'EHL

furniture (n)
los **muebles**
MOO'EH-blays

future (n)
el **futuro**
foo-TOO-ro

frog
la rana

G

globe
el globo terráqueo

game (n)
el **juego**
HOO'AY-go

garage (n)
el **garaje**
gah-RAH-Hay

garden (n)
el **jardín**
Hahr-DEEN

gardener (n)
el **jardinero**
Hahr-dee-NAY-ro

la **jardinera**
Hahr-dee-NAY-rah

gardening (n)
la **jardinería**
Hahr-dee-nay-REE-ah

gas (n)
la **gasolina**
ga-soh-LEE-na

gentle (adj)
suave
SOO'AH-bay

gently (adv)
suavemente
SOO'AH-bay-MEN-tay

giant (n)
el **gigante**
Hee-GAN-tay

giraffe (n)
la **jirafa**
Hee-RAH-fah

girl (n)
la **niña**
NEE-n'ya

la **chica**
CHEE-ka

girlfriend (n)
la **novia**
no-BE'AH

glacier (n)
el **glaciar**
glah-SE'AHR

glass (drink) (n)
el **vaso**
BAH-so

glasses (n)
las **gafas**
GAH-fas

globe (n)
el **globo terráqueo**
GLO-bo tay-RRAH-kay-oh

glove (n)
el **guante**
GOO'AN-tay

glue (n)
la **cola**
KO-la

goal (n)
el **gol**
GOL

goat (n)
la **cabra**
KA-bra

goggles (n)
las **gafas de agua**
GAH-fas day AH-goo'ah

gold (n)
el **oro**
OH-ro

goldfish (n)
el **pececito de colores**
pay-say-SEE-toh day ko-LO-rehs

golf (n)
el **golf**
GOHLF

good (adj)
buen/bueno (m)
BOO'EN/BOO'EH-no

gorilla (n)
el **gorila**
go-REE-la

government (n)
el **gobierno**
go-BE'AIR-no

grandfather (n)
el **abuelo**
ah-BOO'AY-lo

grandmother (n)
la **abuela**
ah-BOO'AY-la

grandparents (n)
los **abuelos**
ah-BOO'AY-los

grape (n)
la **uva**
OO-ba

grass (n)
la **hierba**
YAIR-ba

great (adj)
gran (m)
GRAN

grande (f)
GRAN-day

green (adj)
verde
BAIR-day

greenhouse (n)
el **invernadero**
in-vair-nah-DAY-ro

ground (n)
la **tierra**
TE'AIR-rrah

group (n)
el **grupo**
GROO-po

guide (n)
la **guía**
GHEE-ah

guinea pig (n)
el **conejillo de indias**
ko-nay-HEE-l'yo day IN-de'ahs

guitar (n)
la **guitarra**
ghee-TAH-rrah

gymnastics (n)
la **gimnasia**
Heem-NAH-se'ah

guitar
la guitarra

A B C D E F **G** H I J K L M N O P Q R S T U V W X Y Z

69

H

hamster
el hámster

handbag
el bolso

habitat (n)
el hábitat
AH-be-taht

hair (n)
el pelo
PAY-lo

hair salon (n)
la peluquería
pay-loo-kay-REE-ah

hairbrush (n)
el cepillo de pelo
say-PE-l'yo day PAY-lo

hat
el sombrero

hairy (adj)
peludo (m)
pay-LOO-do

half (n)
la mitad
mee-TAHD

hall (n)
el vestíbulo
bays-TEE-boo-lo

hamster (n)
el hámster
HAHMS-tair

hand (n)
la mano
MAH-no

handbag (n)
el bolso
BOL-so

handkerchief (n)
el pañuelo
pah-N'YU'AY-lo

hang-glider (n)
la ala delta
AH-la DAYL-tah

happy (adj)
feliz
fay-LEES

harbor (n)
el puerto
POO'AIR-to

hard (adj)
duro (m)
DOO-ro

hard drive (n)
el disco duro
DISS-ko DOOR-ro

hare (n)
la liebre
LEE'AY-bray

harvest (n)
la cosecha
ko-SAY-chah

hat (n)
el sombrero
som-BRAY-ro

hawk (n)
el halcón
ahl-KON

hay (n)
el heno
AY-no

he (pron)
él
EL

head (n)
la cabeza
kah-BAY-sa

headache (n)
el dolor de cabeza
doh-LOHR day kah-BAY-sa

healthy (adj)
sano (m)
SAH-no

heart (n)
el corazón
ko-rah-SON

heat (n)
el calor
kah-LOR

heavy (adj)
pesado (m)
pay-SAH-do

helicopter (n)
el helicóptero
eh-lee-KOP-tay-ro

helmet (n)
el casco
KAS-ko

help (n)
la ayuda
ah-YOO-da

her (adj)
su (de ella)
SOO

her (pron)
a ella
ah EH-l'ya

para ella
PAH-ra EH-l'ya

hero (n)
el héroe
EH-ro'eh

la heroína
eh-ro-EE-na

heron (n)
la garza
GAR-sah

hers (pron)
suyo (de ella)
SOO-yo

hi
hola
OH-la

hide-and-seek (n)
las escondidas
ays-kon-DEE-das

high (adj)
alto (m)
AL-to

highway (n)
la autopista
ah'oo-to-PEES-tah

hill (n)
la colina
ko-LEE-na

him (pron)
a él
ah EL

para él
pah-ra EL

hip (n)
la cadera
ka-DAY-ra

his (adj)
su (de él)
SOO

his (pron)
suyo (de él)
SOO-yo

historical (adj)
histórico (m)
iss-TO-re-ko

history (n)
la historia
iss-TO-re'ah

hive (n)
la colmena
kol-MAY-na

hobby (n)
el pasatiempo
pah-sah-TE'EM-po

hockey (n)
el hockey
HOH-kay

hole (n)
el agujero
ah-goo-HAY-ro

home (n)
la casa
KA-sa

homework (n)
la tarea
tah-RAY-ah

honey (n)
la miel
MEE'EL

hood (n)
la capucha
ka-POO-chah

horrible (adj)
horrible
oh-RREE-blay

horse (n)
el caballo
kah-BAH-l'yo

hospital (n)
el hospital
os-pe-TAHL

hot (adj)
caliente
ka-LE'AYN-tay

hot air balloon (n)
el globo aerostático
GLO-bo ah-ay-ros-TAH-te-ko

hot chocolate (n)
el chocolate caliente
cho-ko-LAH-tay ka-LE'AYN-tay

hot dog (n)
el perrito caliente
pay-REE-toh ka-LE'AYN-tay

hotel (n)
el hotel
oh-TEL

hour (n)
la hora
OH-rah

house (n)
la casa
KAH-sah

how (adv)
cómo
KO-mo

huge (adj)
enorme
ay-NOR-may

honey
la miel

human (n)
el humano
oo-MAH-no

hummingbird (n)
el colibrí
ko-le-BREE

hungry (adj)
hambriento (m)
am-BREE'AYN-to

hurricane (n)
el huracán
oo-rah-KAN

husband (n)
el esposo
ess-POH-so

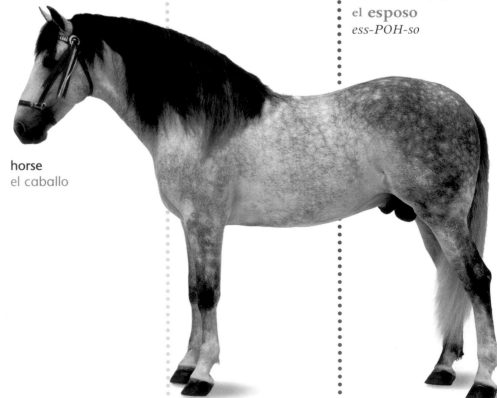

horse
el caballo

A B C D E F G **H** I J K L M N O P Q R S T U V W X Y Z

island
la isla

I (pron)
yo
YO

ice (n)
el hielo
E'AY-lo

ice cream (n)
el helado
eh-LAH-do

ice hockey (n)
el hockey sobre
hielo
HOH-kay so-bray E'AY-lo

ice cream
el helado

ice pop (n)
la paleta
pah-LAY-ta

ice skating (n)
el patinaje sobre
hielo
*pah-te-NAH-Hay
SO-bray E'AY-lo*

idea (n)
la idea
ee-DEH-ah

ill (adj)
enfermo (m)
en-FAIR-mo

illness (n)
la enfermedad
en-fair-may-DAHD

immediately (adv)
inmediatamente
*in-may-DE'AH-tah-
MEN-tay*

important (adj)
importante
im-por-TAN-tay

impossible (adj)
imposible
im-poh-SEE-blay

information (n)
la información
in-for-ma-SE'ON

injury (n)
la lesión
leh-SE'ON

inline skating (n)
el patinaje en
línea
*pah-te-NAH-Hay en
LEE-nee'ah*

insect (n)
el insecto
in-SEK-to

inside (prep)
dentro
DEN-tro

instruction (n)
la instrucción
ins-trook-SE'ON

instrument (n)
el instrumento
ins-troo-MEN-to

interesting (adj)
interesante
in-tay-ray-SAN-tay

international (adj)
internacional
in-tair-nah-se'o-NAHL

Internet (n)
la Internet
In-tair-NEHT

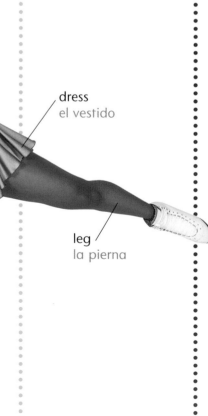

ice skating
el patinaje sobre hielo

dress
el vestido

leg
la pierna

into (prep)
adentro
ah-DEN-tro

dentro
DEN-tro

invitation (n)
la invitación
in-be-tah-SE'ON

iron (clothes) (n)
la plancha
PLAN-chah

island (n)
la isla
EES-lah

it (pron)
ello
EH-l'yo

lo
LOH

its (adj)
su (de ello)
SOO

J

jug
la jarra

jacket (n)
la chaqueta
chah-KAY-ta

jam (n)
la mermelada
mair-meh-LAH-da

jeans (n)
los vaqueros
bah-KAY-ros

jellyfish (n)
la medusa
meh-DOO-sa

jet (n)
el avión
ah-BE'ON

jewel (n)
la joya
HOH-ya

jewelry (n)
la joyería
Hoh-yay-REE-ah

job (n)
el trabajo
tra-BAH-Ho

joke (n)
el chiste
CHEES-tay

judo (n)
el judo
JOO-do

jug (n)
la jarra
HAR-rrah

juice (n)
el jugo
HOO-go

jump rope (n)
la cuerda de saltar
KOO'AIR-da day
sal-TAR

jungle (n)
la jungla
HOON-glah

just (adv)
sólo
SOH-lo

jeans
los vaqueros

K

kite
la cometa

kangaroo (n)
el canguro
kan-GOO-ro

karate (n)
el karate
ka-RAH-tay

kettle (n)
el hervidor
air-BE-dor

key (n)
la llave
L'YA-bay

keyboard (n)
el teclado
tay-KLA-do

kind (gentle) (adj)
amable
ah-MAH-blay

kind (type) (n)
el tipo
TEE-po

king (n)
el rey
RRAY

kiss (n)
el beso
BAY-so

kitchen (n)
la cocina
ko-SEE-na

kite (n)
la cometa
ko-MAY-ta

kitten (n)
el gatito
gah-TEE-to

knee (n)
la rodilla
rroh-DEE-l'ya

knife (n)
el cuchillo
koo-CHEE-l'yo

knight (n)
el caballero
kah-bah-L'YAY-ro

knot (n)
el nudo
NOO-do

koala (n)
el koala
ko-AH-la

tail
la cola

kitten
el gatito

A B C D E F G H I J K L M N O P Q R S T U V W X Y Z

L

lemon
el limón

ladder (n)
la escalera
ess-kah-LAY-rah

ladybug (n)
la mariquita
mah-ree-KEE-ta

lake (n)
el lago
LAH-go

lamb (n)
el cordero
kor-DAY-roh

lamp (n)
la lámpara
LAM-pah-rah

land (n)
la tierra
TE'AY-rrah

language (n)
el idioma
e-DEE'OH-ma

laptop (n)
la computadora
portátil
kom-poo-tah-DOO-rah
pohr-TAH-teel

last (adj)
último (m)
OOL-te-mo

late (adv)
tarde
TAHR-day

law (n)
la ley
LAY

lawn (n)
el césped
SESS-payd

lawn mower (n)
el cortacésped
kor-tah-SESS-payd

layer (n)
la capa
KAH-pa

lazy (adj)
perezoso (m)
pay-ray-SOH-so

leaf (n)
la hoja
OH-Hah

leather (n)
el cuero
KOO'AY-roh

left (side) (n)
la izquierda
lis-KE'AIR-da

left-handed (adj)
zurdo (m)
SOOR-doh

leg (n)
la pierna
PE'AIR-nah

lemon (n)
el limón
lee-MON

lemonade (n)
la limonada
lee-mo-NAH-da

leopard (n)
el leopardo
lay-oh-PAHR-do

lesson (n)
la lección
lek-SE'ON

letter (alphabet) (n)
la letra
LAY-trah

letter (mail) (n)
la carta
KAR-tah

lettuce (n)
la lechuga
lay-CHOO-gah

level (n)
el nivel
nee-BEL

library (n)
la biblioteca
be-ble'oh-TAY-ka

lid (n)
la tapa
TAH-pah

life (n)
la vida
BEE-dah

lifeboat (n)
el bote salvavidas
BO-tay sal-bah-BEE-das

lifeguard (n)
el salvavidas
sal-bah-BEE-das

life jacket (n)
el chaleco
salvavidas
chah-LAY-ko
sal-bah-BEE-das

light (n)
la luz
LOOS

light (in color) (adj)
claro (m)
KLAH-ro

light (in weight) (adj)
ligero (m)
lee-HAY-ro

light bulb (n)
la bombilla
bohm-BEE-l'ya

lighthouse (n)
el faro
FAH-ro

lightning (n)
el relámpago
ray-LAM-pah-go

like (prep)
como
KOH-mo

line (n)
la línea
LEE-nay'ah

lion (n)
el león
lay-ON

lipstick (n)
el lápiz de labios
LAH-pis day LAH-be'os

liquid (n)
el líquido
LEE-ke-do

list (n)
la lista
LEES-tah

little (adj)
pequeño (m)
pay-KAY-n'yo

living room (n)
la sala
SAH-la

lizard
el lagarto

74

lizard (n)
el lagarto
lah-GAR-to

lobster (n)
la langosta
lan-GOSS-ta

location (n)
la ubicación
oo-be-ka-SE'ON

long (adj)
largo (m)
LAHR-go

loop (n)
el lazo
LA-sso

loose (adj)
suelto (m)
SOO'ELL-to

(a) lot (adj)
mucho (m)
MOO-choh

loud (adj)
alto (m)
AHL-to

lovely (adj)
encantador (m)
en-kan-tah-DOR

low (adj)
bajo (m)
BAH-Hoh

lucky (adj)
afortunado (m)
ah-for-too-NAH-do

luggage (n)
el equipaje
eh-kee-PAH-Heh

lunch (n)
el almuerzo
al-MO'AIR-soh

lunch box (n)
la lonchera
lohn-CHAY-rah

mask
la máscara

machine (n)
la máquina
MAH-kee-na

magazine (n)
la revista
ray-BES-tah

magician (n)
el mago
MAH-go

magnet (n)
el imán
e-MAHN

magnetic (adj)
magnético (m)
mag-NEH-te-ko

magnifying glass (n)
la lupa
LOO-pa

mail (n)
el correo
ko-RRAY'OH

mail carrier (n)
el cartero
kar-TAY-roh

la cartera
kar-TAY-rah

mailbox (n)
el buzón
boo-SON

main (adj)
principal
preen-se-PAL

make-up (n)
el maquillaje
mah-kee-L'YAH-Heh

male (n)
el varón
bah-RON

mammal (n)
el mamífero
mah-MEE-fay-ro

man (n)
el hombre
OM-bray

map (n)
el mapa
MAH-pa

marble (toy) (n)
la canica
ka-NEE-kah

mark (n)
la marca
MAR-ka

marker (n)
el marcador
mahr-ka-DOR

market (n)
el mercado
mair-KAH-do

married (adj)
casado (m)
ka-SAH-do

mask (n)
la máscara
MAHS-kah-rah

mat (n)
el felpudo
fell-POO-do

match (n)
el partido
pahr-TE-do

matchbox (n)
la caja de cerillas
KAH-Ha day
say-REE-l'yahs

math (n)
las matemáticas
mah-tay-MAH-tee-kas

maybe (adv)
quizás
kee-SASS

tal vez
tahl BESS

me (pron)
me
MAY

a mí
ah MEE

meal (n)
la comida
ko-ME-da

meaning (n)
el significado
seeg-nee-fee-KAH-do

measurement (n)
la medida
may-DEE-da

meat (n)
la carne
KAR-nay

melon
el melón

A B C D E F G H I J K **L M** N O P Q R S T U V W X Y Z

A B C D E F G H I J K L **M** N O P Q R S T U V W X Y Z

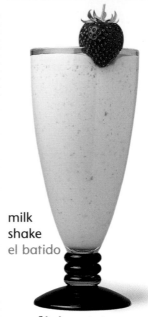

milk
shake
el batido

medicine (n)
la medicina
may-de-SEE-na

melon (n)
el melón
may-LON

menu (n)
el menú
may-NOO

mess (n)
el lío
LEE-oh

message (n)
el mensaje
men-SAH-He

metal (n)
el metal
may-TAHL

microwave (n)
el microondas
mee-kroh-ON-dahs

middle (n)
el medio
MEH-de'oh

midnight (n)
la medianoche
MEH-de'ah-NO-chay

milk (n)
la leche
LAY-chay

milk shake (n)
el batido
bah-TEE-do

million
millón
mee-L'YON

mineral (n)
el mineral
mee-nay-RAHL

minute (time) (n)
el minuto
mee-NOO-to

mirror (n)
el espejo
ess-PAY-Ho

mistake (n)
el error
eh-RROR

mitten (n)
la manopla
mah-NOH-pla

mixture (n)
la mezcla
MES-kla

modeling clay (n)
la plastilina
plas-te-LEE-na

mom (n)
la mamá
mah-MAH

money (n)
el dinero
de-NAY-roh

monkey (n)
el mono
MOH-no

mitten
la manopla

monster (n)
el monstruo
mons-troo-oh

month (n)
el mes
MESS

moon (n)
la luna
LOO-na

more than
más de
MAHS day

morning (n)
la mañana
mah-N'YA-na

moth (n)
la polilla
poh-LEE-l'ya

mother (n)
la madre
MAH-dray

motor (n)
el motor
MOH-tor

motorcycle (n)
la motocicleta
mo-to-see-KLAY-tah

mountain (n)
la montaña
mon-TAH-n'ya

mountain bike (n)
la bicicleta de
montaña
*be-se-KLAY-tah day
mon-TAH-n'ya*

mouse (animal) (n)
el ratón
rah-TON

**mouse (computer)
(n)**
el ratón
rah-TON

mouse pad (n)
la alfombrilla
del ratón
*ahl-FOM-bree-l'ya
dell rah-TON*

moustache (n)
el bigote
be-GOH-tay

mouth (n)
la boca
BOH-ka

movie (n)
la película
pay-LE-koo-lah

mud (n)
el barro
BAH-rro

muddy (adj)
enfangado (m)
en-fan-GAH-do

mug (n)
la taza
TAH-sa

museum (n)
el museo
moo-SAY-oh

mushroom (n)
el hongo
ON-go

music (n)
la música
MOO-see-ka

musician (n)
el músico
MOO-see-ko

la música
MOO-see-ka

my (adj)
mi/mis (sing/plu)
MEE/MEES

mushroom
el hongo

N

necklace
el collar

nail (n)
la uña
OO-n'ya

name (n)
el nombre
NOM-bray

narrow (adj)
estrecho (m)
ess-TRAY-choh

national (adj)
nacional
na-se'oh-NAHL

nature (n)
la naturaleza
nah-too-rah-LAY-sah

naughty (adj)
travieso (m)
trah-bee-AY-soh

nest
el nido

near (adv)
cerca
SAIR-kah

nearly (adv)
casi
KAH-see

neck (n)
el cuello
KOO'EH-l'yo

necklace (n)
el collar
koh-L'YAR

needle (n)
la aguja
ah-GOO-Ha

neighbor (n)
el vecino
beh-SEE-no

la vecina
beh-SEE-nah

neighborhood (n)
el barrio
BA-rre'oh

nephew (n)
el sobrino
soh-BREE-no

nest (n)
el nido
NEE-doh

net (n)
la red
RRED

never (adv)
nunca
NOON-ka

new (adj)
nuevo (m)
NOO'AY-bo

news (n)
la noticia
no-tee-SEE'AH

newspaper (n)
el periódico
pay-ree-OH-de-ko

next (adj)
siguiente
see-GHEE'EN-tay

nice (adj)
bonito (m)
boh-NEE-toh

niece (n)
la sobrina
soh-BREE-na

night (n)
la noche
NOH-chay

nobody (pron)
nadie
nah-DE'AY

noisy (adj)
ruidoso (m)
roo'ee-DO-so

noodle (n)
el fideo
fee-DAY-oh

north (n)
el norte
NOR-tay

nose (n)
la nariz
nah-REES

note (n)
la nota
NO-tah

notebook (n)
la libreta
lee-BRAY-tah

noodles
los fideos

nothing (pron)
nada
NAH-dah

now (adv)
ahora
ah-OH-rah

nowhere (adv)
en ninguna parte
en neen-GOO-nah PAIR-tay

number (n)
el número
NOO-may-roh

nurse (n)
el enfermero
en-fair-MAY-ro

la enfermera
en-fair-MAY-ra

nursery (n)
el cuarto de los niños
KOO'AR-toh day loss NEE-n'yos

marker
el marcador

notebook
la libreta

A B C D E F G H I J K L M N O P Q R S T U V W X Y Z

O

ocean
el océano

oar (n)
el remo
RAY-moh

object (n)
el objeto
ob-HAY-to

ocean (n)
el océano
oh-SAY-ah-no

office (n)
la oficina
oh-fee-SEE-na

often (adv)
a menudo
ah may-NOO-do

onion
la cebolla

oil (n)
el aceite
ah-SAY'EE-tay

old (adj)
viejo (m)
BE'AY-Ho

old person (n)
el anciano
ahn-SEE'AH-no

la anciana
ahn-SEE'AH-na

Olympic Games (n)
los Juegos
Olímpicos
HOO'AY-gos
oh-LEEM-pe-kos

on top of (prep)
encima de
en-SEE-mah day

onion (n)
la cebolla
say-BOH-l'yah

only (adv)
sólo
soh-lo

open (adj)
abierto (m)
ah-BE'AIR-toh

opening hours (n)
el horario
oh-RAH-re'oh

orange
la naranja

orange juice
el jugo de naranja

operation (n)
la operación
oh-pay-rah-SE'ON

opposite (adj)
opuesto (m)
oh-POO'AYS-toh

or (conj)
o
OH

orange (color) (adj)
anaranjado (m)
ah-nah-ran-HAH-do

orange (fruit) (n)
la naranja
nah-RAHN-Hah

orange juice (n)
el jugo de naranja
HOO-goh day
nah-RAHN-Hah

orchestra (n)
la orquesta
or-KAYS-tah

other (adj)
otro (m)
OH-troh

Ouch!
¡Ay!
AY

our (adj)
nuestro/nuestros
(m, sing/plu)
noo-AYS-troh/
noo-AYS-tros

nuestra/nuestras
(f, sing/plu)
noo-AYS-trah/
noo-AYS-tras

out of (prep)
fuera de
FOO'AY-rah day

outside (adv)
fuera
FOO'AY-rah

oval (n)
el óvalo
OH-bah-lo

oven (n)
el horno
OHR-no

oven mitt (n)
la manopla
mah-NO-plah

over there (adv)
allí
ah-L'YEE

allá
ah-L'YAH

owl (n)
el búho
BOO-oh

own (adj)
propio (m)
PROH-pe'oh

owl
el búho

P

paint can
la lata de pintura

page (n)
la página
PAH-Hee-na

paint brush (n)
el pincel
peen-SELL

paint can (n)
la lata de pintura
LAH-ta day
peen-TOO-rah

painting (n)
la pintura
peen-TOO-rah

pair (n)
la pareja
pah-RAY-Ha

pajamas (n)
el pijama
pee-HAH-ma

palm tree (n)
la palmera
pal-MAY-ra

pancake (n)
el panqueque
pan-KAY-kay

panda (n)
el panda
PAHN-dah

pants (n)
los pantalones
pan-ta-LOH-ness

paper (n)
el papel
pah-PEL

paper towel (n)
la servilleta
de papel
sair-bee-L'YEH-tah day
PAH-pel

parade (n)
el desfile
des-FEE-lay

parents (n)
los padres
PAH-dress

park (n)
el parque
PAHR-kay

parrot (n)
el loro
LOH-roh

part (n)
la parte
PAR-tay

party (n)
la fiesta
FEE'AYS-tah

passenger (n)
el pasajero
pah-sah-HAY-ro
la pasajera
pah-sah-HAY-ra

passport (n)
el pasaporte
pah-sah-POR-tay

past (n)
el pasado
pah-SAH-do

past (prep)
después (de)
des-POO'AYS (day)

pasta (n)
la pasta
PAS-tah

path (n)
el sendero
sen-DAY-ro

patient (adj)
paciente
pah-SEE'EN-tay

patient (n)
el paciente
pah-SEE'EN-tay
la paciente
pah-SEE'EN-tay

pattern (n)
el patrón
pah-TRON

paw (n)
la pata
PAH-ta

pay (n)
el salario
sah-LAH-re'o

pea (n)
el guisante
ghee-SAN-tay

peace (n)
la paz
PAS

peaceful (adj)
tranquilo (m)
tran-KEE-lo

peanut (n)
el cacahuate
kah-ka-OO'AH-tay

pear
la pera

pear (n)
la pera
PAY-ra

pebble (n)
el guijarro
ghee-HAH-rro

pedal (n)
el pedal
pay-DAHL

pelican (n)
el pelícano
pay-LEE-kah-no

pen (n)
la pluma
PLOO-mah

pencil (n)
el lápiz
LAH-pis

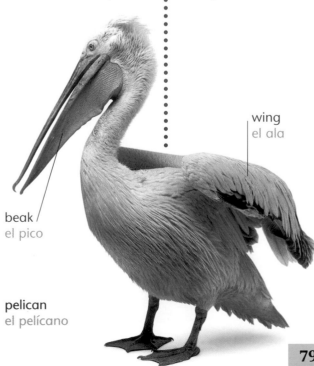

wing
el ala

beak
el pico

pelican
el pelícano

A B C D E F G H I J K L M N O **P** Q R S T U V W X Y Z

79

pencil case (n)
el **plumier**
ploo-MEE'AIR

penguin (n)
el **pingüino**
peen-GOO'E-no

people (n)
la **gente**
HEN-tay

pepper (n)
la **pimienta**
pe-ME'EN-tah

perfect (adj)
perfecto (m)
pair-FEK-toh

perhaps (adv)
quizá
kee-SAH

quizás
kee-SASS

person (n)
la **persona**
pair-SOH-na

pet (n)
la **mascota**
mass-KOH-ta

piano
el piano

pharmacist (n)
el **farmacéutico**
far-mah-SAY'OO-te-ko

la **farmacéutica**
far-mah-SAY'OO-te-ka

phone (n)
el **teléfono**
tay-LAY-fo-no

photo (n)
la **foto**
FOH-to

phrase (n)
la **frase**
FRAH-say

piano (n)
el **piano**
PE'AH-no

picnic (n)
el **picnic**
PEEK-neek

picture (n)
el **dibujo**
de-BOO-Ho

pinecone
la piña

piece (n)
la **pieza**
PE'AY-sah

pig (n)
el **cerdo**
SAIR-do

pillow (n)
la **almohada**
al-moh'AH-da

pilot (n)
el/la **piloto**
pe-LOH-to

pine tree (n)
el **pino**
PEE-no

pineapple (n)
la **piña**
PEE-n'ya

pinecone (n)
la **piña**
PEE-n'ya

pink (adj)
rosa
RROH-sa

pizza (n)
la **pizza**
PEET-sa

place (n)
el **lugar**
loo-GAR

plane (n)
el **avión**
ah-BEE'ON

planet (n)
el **planeta**
plah-NAY-ta

plant (n)
la **planta**
PLAHN-ta

plastic (adj)
plástico (m)
PLASS-te-ko

plastic bag (n)
la **bolsa de plástico**
BOL-sah day PLASS-te-ko

plate (n)
el **plato**
PLAH-to

platform (n)
la **plataforma**
plah-ta-FOR-ma

play (n)
el **juego**
HOO'AY-go

player (n)
el **jugador**
Hoo-gah-DOR

la **jugadora**
Hoo-gah-DO-ra

pine tree
el pino

playground (n)
el parque infantil
PAHR-kay in-fan-TEEL

playtime (n)
el recreo
ray-KRAY-oh

please (adv)
por favor
POR fah-VOR

plug (n)
el enchufe
en-CHOO-fay

pocket (n)
el bolsillo
bol-SEE-l'yo

pocket money (n)
la semanada
say-mah-NAH-da

point (n)
el punto
POON-to

pointed (adj)
puntiagudo (m)
poon-te'ah-GOO-do

polar bear (n)
el oso polar
O-so poh-LAR

pole (n)
el polo
POH-lo

police (n)
la policía
poh-le-SEE-ah

police car (n)
el coche de policía
KO-chay day
poh-le-SEE-ah

police helicopter (n)
el helicóptero de la policía
eh-le-KOP-tay-ro day
lah poh-le-SEE-ah

pollution (n)
la polución
poh-loo-SE'ON

pond (n)
el estanque
es-TAN-kay

poor (adj)
pobre
POH-bray

popular (adj)
popular
po-poo-LAHR

possible (adj)
posible
po-SEE-blay

post office (n)
la oficina de correos
o-fe-SEE-nah day
ko-RRAY-ohs

postcard (n)
la postal
pos-TAHL

poster (n)
el cartel
kar-TELL

potato (n)
la papa
PA-pa

pouch (n)
la bolsa
BOL-sah

powder (n)
el polvo
POHL-boh

present (n)
el regalo
ray-GAH-lo

president (n)
el presidente
pray-see-DEN-tay
la presidenta
pray-see-DEN-tah

puppet
la marioneta

pretty (adj)
bonito (m)
boh-NEE-toh

price (n)
el precio
PRAY-se'oh

prince (n)
el príncipe
PREEN-se-pay

princess (n)
la princesa
preen-SAY-sah

prize (n)
el premio
PRAY-me'oh

probably (adv)
probablemente
pro-BAH-blay-MEN-tay

problem (n)
el problema
pro-BLAY-mah

program (n)
el programa
pro-GRAH-ma

project (n)
el proyecto
pro-YEHK-to

pudding (n)
el pudin
POO-deen

pumpkin (n)
la calabaza
ka-la-BAH-sa

puppet (n)
la marioneta
mah-re'oh-NAY-ta

puppet show (n)
el espectáculo de marionetas
ess-pehk-TAH-koo-lo day
mah-re'oh-NAY-ta

puppy (n)
el perrito
pair-RREE-to

purple (adj)
violeta
be'oh-LAY-la

purse (n)
el bolso
BOL-so

puzzle (n)
el rompecabezas
rrom-pay-kah-BAY-sas

purse
el bolso

A
B
C
D
E
F
G
H
I
J
K
L
M
N
O
P
Q
R
S
T
U
V
W
X
Y
Z

A B C D E F G H I J K L M N O P **Q R** S T U V W X Y Z

Q R

quarter (n)
el cuarto
KOO'AR-toh

queen (n)
la reina
RRAY-na

question (n)
la pregunta
preh-GOON-tah

quickly (adv)
deprisa
day-PREE-sa

quiet (adj)
tranquilo (m)
tran-KEE-lo

quietly (adv)
sin hacer ruido
SIN ah-SAIR roo'ee-DO

quiz (n)
la prueba
PROO'AY-ba

racing car
el coche de carreras

rabbit (n)
el conejo
ko-NAY-ho

race (n)
la carrera
ka-RRAY-ra

racing car (n)
el coche de
carreras
*KO-chay day
ka-RRAY-ras*

racket (n)
la raqueta
rrah-KAY-ta

radio (n)
la radio
RRAH-de'oh

railway station (n)
la estación de tren
ess-tah-SE'ON day TREN

rain (n)
la lluvia
LYU-be'ah

rain forest (n)
la selva tropical
SELL-bah tro-pe-KAHL

queen
la reina

rainbow (n)
el arcoiris
ar-ko-EE-ris

raincoat (n)
el chubasquero
choo-bas-KAY-roh

rake (n)
el rastrillo
rrass-TREE-l'yo

raspberry (n)
la frambuesa
fram-boo'AY-sa

rat (n)
la rata
RRAH-ta

reading (n)
la lectura
lek-TOO-ra

ready (adj)
listo (m)
LEES-to

real (adj)
real
rray-AHL

really (adv)
realmente
rray-AHL-MEN-tay

receipt (n)
el recibo
rray-SE-bo

recipe (n)
la receta
rray-SAY-ta

rectangle (n)
el rectángulo
rrehk-TAN-goo-lo

red (adj)
rojo (m)
RROH-Ho

remote control (n)
el mando a
distancia
*MAN-do ah
dees-TAN-se'ah*

report (n)
el informe
in-FOR-may

rescue (n)
el rescate
rress-KAH-tay

restaurant (n)
el restaurante
ress-ta'oo-RAN-tay

rhinoceros (n)
el rinoceronte
rree-no-say-RON-tay

ribbon (n)
la cinta
SEEN-tah

rice (n)
el arroz
ah-RROS

rich (adj)
rico (m)
RREE-koh

right (side) (n)
la derecha
day-RAY-chah

right (correct) (adj)
correcto (m)
kor-RREK-to

S

saddle
la silla de montar

ring (n)
el anillo
ah-NEE-l'yo

ripe (adj)
maduro (m)
mah-DOO-ro

river (n)
el río
REE-oh

road (n)
el camino
ka-MEE-no

robot (n)
el robot
rro-BOT

rock (n)
la roca
ROH-ka

rocket (n)
el cohete
ko-AY-tay

roll (n)
el panecillo
pah-neh-SEE-l'yo

roller skating (n)
el patinaje
pah-tee-NAH-hay

roof (n)
el tejado
tay-HA-do

room (n)
el cuarto
KOO'AR-toh

root (n)
la raíz
rah-EES

rope (n)
la cuerda
KOO-AIR-da

rose (n)
la rosa
RROH-sa

rough (adj)
rugoso (m)
rroo-GO-so

round (adj)
redondo (m)
rray-DON-do

roundabout (n)
la rueda
RROO'AY-dah

route (n)
la ruta
ROO-ta

row boat (n)
el bote de remos
BOH-tay day REH-mos

rubber band (n)
el elástico
eh-LAHS-te-ko

rug (n)
el tapete
tah-PAY-tay

rugby (n)
el rugby
RROOG-be

ruler (measuring) (n)
la regla
RAY-glah

sack (n)
el saco
SAH-ko

sad (adj)
triste
TRISS-tay

saddle (n)
la silla de montar
SEE-l'yah day mon-TAR

safe (adj)
seguro (m)
say-GOO-ro

sail (n)
la vela
BAY-la

sailboat (n)
el velero
bay-LAY-ro

sailing (n)
navegar
na-bay-GAR

sailor (n)
el marinero
mah-ree-NAY-ro

salad (n)
la ensalada
en-sa-LAH-da

salt (n)
la sal
SAHL

same (adj)
mismo (m)
MEES-moh

sand (n)
la arena
ah-RAY-na

sandal (n)
la sandalia
san-DAH-le'ah

sandcastle (n)
el castillo de arena
kass-TEE-l'yo day
ah-RAY-na

sandwich (n)
el sándwich
SAHND-oo'ich

saucepan (n)
el cazo
KAH-so

scarf (n)
la bufanda
boo-FAHN-da

school (n)
la escuela
ess-KOO'AY-la

school bag (n)
la bolsa de la
escuela
BOL-sah day la
ess-KOO'AY-la

school uniform (n)
el uniforme escolar
oo-nee-FOHR-may
ess-ko-LAR

scarf
la bufanda

A B C D E F G H I J K L M N O P Q **R** **S** T U V W X Y Z

83

A B C D E F G H I J K L M N O P Q R **S** T U V W X Y Z

scissors
las tijeras

science (n)
las ciencias
SEE'EN-see'as

scientist (n)
el científico
see'ehn-TEE-fee-ko

la científica
see'ehn-TEE-fee-ka

scissors (n)
las tijeras
tee-HAY-ras

score (n)
el puntaje
poon-TAH-Hay

screen (n)
la pantalla
pan-TAH-l'ya

sea (n)
el mar
MAHR

sea lion (n)
el león marino
lay-ON ma-REE-no

seafood (n)
el marisco
ma-REES-ko

seagull (n)
la gaviota
ga-be-OH-ta

seal (n)
la foca
FOH-ka

seaside (n)
la orilla del mar
o-REE-l'ya dell MAHR

season (n)
la estación
ess-tah-SE'ON

seaweed (n)
el alga
AHL-ga

second (adj)
segundo (m)
say-GOON-do

seed (n)
la semilla
say-MEE-l'ya

semicircle (n)
el semicírculo
say-me-SEER-koo-lo

sense (n)
el sentido
sen-TEE-do

shadow (n)
la sombra
SOHM-bra

shallow (adj)
poco profundo (m)
POH-ko pro-FOON-do

shampoo (n)
el champú
cham-POO

shape (n)
la figura
fe-GOO-ra

shark (n)
el tiburón
te-boo-RON

sharp (adj)
afilado (m)
a-fee-LAH-do

she (pron)
ella
eh-l'ya

sheep (n)
la oveja
o-BAY-Hah

sheepdog (n)
el perro pastor
PAIR-rro pass-TOR

sheet (on bed) (n)
la sábana
SAH-ba-na

shelf (n)
el estante
ess-TAHN-tay

shell (n)
la concha
KOHN-cha

shiny (adj)
brillante
bree-L'YAN-tay

ship (n)
el barco
BAR-ko

shirt (n)
la camisa
ka-MEE-sa

shoe (n)
el zapato
sa-PAH-to

shop (n)
la tienda
TEE'AYN-da

wool
la lana

sheep
las ovejas

shopkeeper (n)
el vendedor
ben-day-DOR

la vendedora
ben-day-dor-RAH

shopper (n)
el cliente
klee-EN-tay

la clienta
klee-EN-tah

shopping bag (n)
la bolsa de la
compra
*BOL-sah day la
KOM-prah*

shopping cart (n)
el carrito de
compras
*ka-RREE-toh day
KOM-prahs*

shopping list (n)
la lista de la
compra
*LEES-tah day la
KOM-prah*

shore (n)
la costa
KOSS-tah

short (adj)
corto (m)
KOR-to

shorts (n)
los pantalones
cortos
*pan-ta-LOH-ness
KOR-tos*

shoulder (n)
el hombro
OM-bro

shovel (n)
la pala
PAH-la

show (n)
el espectáculo
ess-pehk-TAH-koo-lo

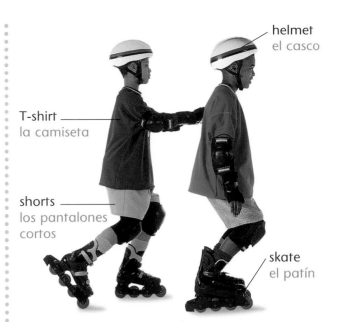

helmet
el casco

T-shirt
la camiseta

shorts
los pantalones
cortos

skate
el patín

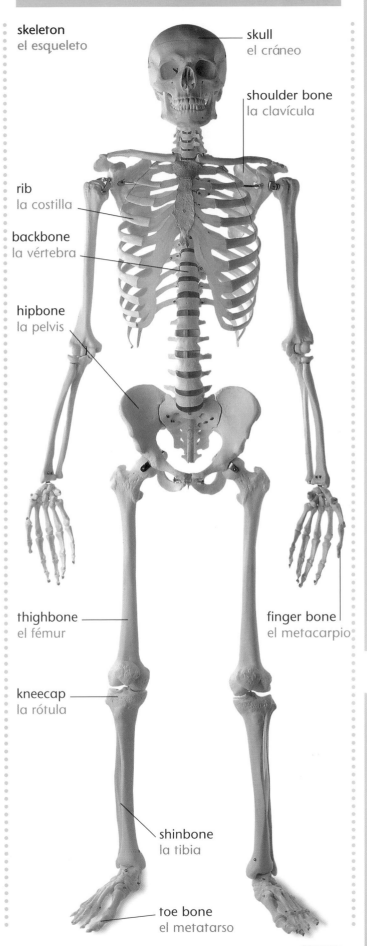

skeleton
el esqueleto

skull
el cráneo

shoulder bone
la clavícula

rib
la costilla

backbone
la vértebra

hipbone
la pelvis

thighbone
el fémur

finger bone
el metacarpio

kneecap
la rótula

shinbone
la tibia

toe bone
el metatarso

shower (n)
la **ducha**
DOO-chah

shy (adj)
tímido (m)
TEE-me-do

sick (adj)
enfermo (m)
en-FAIR-mo

sidewalk (n)
el **pavimento**
pah-be-MEN-to

sign (n)
la **señal**
say-N'YAL

simple (adj)
sencillo (m)
sen-SEE-l'yo

sink (bathroom) (n)
el **lavabo**
lah-BAH-bo

sink (kitchen) (n)
el **fregadero**
fray-ga-DEH-ro

sister (n)
la **hermana**
air-MAH-nah

size (n)
el **tamaño**
ta-MAH-n'yo

skate (n)
el **patín**
pa-TEEN

skateboard (n)
el **monopatín**
mo-no-pa-TEEN

skating (n)
el **patinaje**
pa-te-NAH-Hay

skeleton (n)
el **esqueleto**
ess-kay-LEH-to

ski (n)
el **esquí**
ess-KEE

skin (n)
la **piel**
PE'AYL

skirt (n)
la **falda**
FAHL-da

sky (n)
el **cielo**
SEE'AY-lo

skyscraper (n)
el **rascacielos**
rass-ka-SEE'AY-los

sled (n)
el **trineo**
tree-NAY-oh

A
B
C
D
E
F
G
H
I
J
K
L
M
N
O
P
Q
R
S
T
U
V
W
X
Y
Z

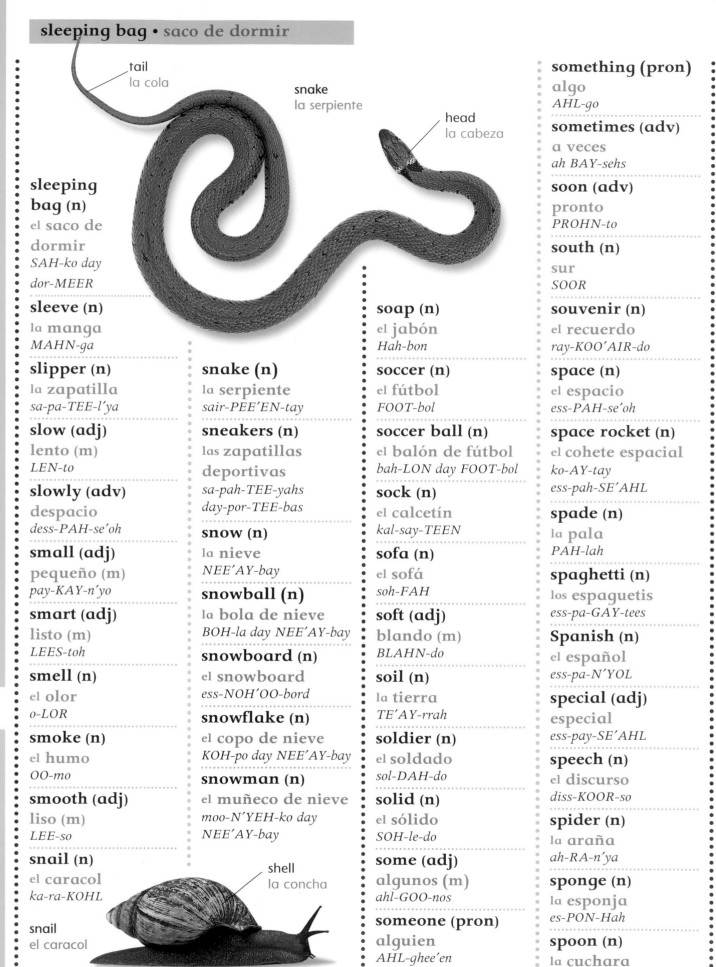

tail
la cola

snake
la serpiente

head
la cabeza

shell
la concha

snail
el caracol

sleeping bag (n)
el saco de dormir
SAH-ko day dor-MEER

sleeve (n)
la manga
MAHN-ga

slipper (n)
la zapatilla
sa-pa-TEE-l'ya

slow (adj)
lento (m)
LEN-to

slowly (adv)
despacio
dess-PAH-se'oh

small (adj)
pequeño (m)
pay-KAY-n'yo

smart (adj)
listo (m)
LEES-toh

smell (n)
el olor
o-LOR

smoke (n)
el humo
OO-mo

smooth (adj)
liso (m)
LEE-so

snail (n)
el caracol
ka-ra-KOHL

snake (n)
la serpiente
sair-PEE'EN-tay

sneakers (n)
las zapatillas deportivas
sa-pah-TEE-yahs day-por-TEE-bas

snow (n)
la nieve
NEE'AY-bay

snowball (n)
la bola de nieve
BOH-la day NEE'AY-bay

snowboard (n)
el snowboard
ess-NOH'OO-bord

snowflake (n)
el copo de nieve
KOH-po day NEE'AY-bay

snowman (n)
el muñeco de nieve
moo-N'YEH-ko day NEE'AY-bay

soap (n)
el jabón
Hah-bon

soccer (n)
el fútbol
FOOT-bol

soccer ball (n)
el balón de fútbol
bah-LON day FOOT-bol

sock (n)
el calcetín
kal-say-TEEN

sofa (n)
el sofá
soh-FAH

soft (adj)
blando (m)
BLAHN-do

soil (n)
la tierra
TE'AY-rrah

soldier (n)
el soldado
sol-DAH-do

solid (n)
el sólido
SOH-le-do

some (adj)
algunos (m)
ahl-GOO-nos

someone (pron)
alguien
AHL-ghee'en

something (pron)
algo
AHL-go

sometimes (adv)
a veces
ah BAY-sehs

soon (adv)
pronto
PROHN-to

south (n)
sur
SOOR

souvenir (n)
el recuerdo
ray-KOO'AIR-do

space (n)
el espacio
ess-PAH-se'oh

space rocket (n)
el cohete espacial
ko-AY-tay ess-pah-SE'AHL

spade (n)
la pala
PAH-lah

spaghetti (n)
los espaguetis
ess-pa-GAY-tees

Spanish (n)
el español
ess-pa-N'YOL

special (adj)
especial
ess-pay-SE'AHL

speech (n)
el discurso
diss-KOOR-so

spider (n)
la araña
ah-RA-n'ya

sponge (n)
la esponja
es-PON-Hah

spoon (n)
la cuchara
koo-CHAH-ra

A B C D E F G H I J K L M N O P Q R **S** T U V W X Y Z

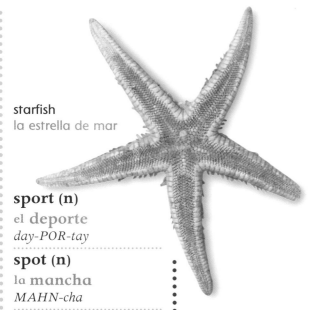

starfish
la estrella de mar

sport (n)
el deporte
day-POR-tay

spot (n)
la mancha
MAHN-cha

spring (season) (n)
la primavera
pree-ma-BAY-ra

square (n)
el cuadrado
koo'ah-DRAH-do

squirrel (n)
la ardilla
air-DEE-l'ya

stairs (n)
las escaleras
ess-kah-LAY-ras

stamp (n)
el sello
SAY-l'yo

star (n)
la estrella
ess-TRAY-l'ya

starfish (n)
la estrella de mar
ess-TRAY-l'ya
day MAHR

station (n)
la estación
ess-tah-SE'ON

statue (n)
la estatua
ess-TAH-too'ah

steam (n)
el vapor
bah-POR

steep (adj)
empinado (m)
em-pee-NAH-do

stem (n)
el tallo
TAH-l'yo

step (n)
el paso
PAH-so

stepfather (n)
el padrastro
pah-DRAHS-tro

stepmother (n)
la madrastra
mah-DRAHS-tra

stick (n)
el palo
PAH-lo

sticker (n)
la pegatina
pay-gah-TEE-na

sticky (adj)
pegajoso (m)
pay-gah-HOH-so

still (adj)
quieto (m)
KEE'AY-to

stocking (n)
la media
MAY-de'ah

stomach (n)
el estómago
ess-TOH-ma-go

stone (n)
la piedra
PEE'AY-dra

stormy (adj)
tempestuoso (m)
tem-pess-too-OH-so

story (n)
el cuento
KOO'EN-to

stove (n)
la cocina
ko-SEE-na

straight (adj)
recto (m)
RREK-to

strange (adj)
extraño (m)
eks-TRAH-n'yo

straw (n)
la paja
PAH-haa

strawberry (n)
la fresa
FRAY-sa

street (n)
la calle
KAH-l'ye

strict (adj)
estricto (m)
ess-TREEK-to

string (n)
la cuerda
KOO'AIR-da

stripe (n)
la raya
RRAH-yah

strawberry
la fresa

strong (adj)
fuerte
FOO'AIR-tay

student (n)
el/la estudiante
ess-too-DEE'AHN-tay

stupid (adj)
estúpido (m)
ess-TOO-pe-do

subject (n)
la materia
mah-TEH-re'ah

submarine (n)
el submarino
soob-mah-REE-no

subway (n)
el metro
MAY-tro

suddenly (adv)
de repente
day ray-PEN-tay

sugar (n)
el azúcar
ah-SOO-kar

suit (n)
el traje
TRAH-Hay

suitcase (n)
la maleta
ma-LAY-ta

summer (n)
el verano
bay-RAH-no

summit (n)
la cumbre
KOOM-bray

sunflower
el girasol

A B C D E F G H I J K L M N O P Q R **S** T U V W X Y Z

sun (n)
el **sol**
SOHL

sunblock (n)
el **protector solar**
pro-tehk-TOR so-LAR

sunflower (n)
el **girasol**
Hee-ra-SOHL

sunglasses (n)
las **gafas de sol**
GAH-fas day SOHL

sunhat (n)
la **pamela**
pa-MAY-la

sunlight (n)
la **luz del sol**
LOOS dell SOHL

sunny (adj)
soleado (m)
so-lay-AH-do

sunset (n)
el **atardecer**
ah-tar-day-SAIR

supermarket (n)
el **supermercado**
soo-pair-mair-KAH-do

sure (adj)
seguro (m)
say-GOO-ro

swing
el columpio

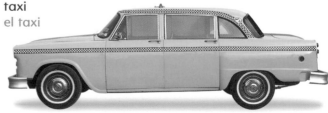

surface (n)
la **superficie**
soo-pair-FEE-ce'eh

surfboard (n)
la **tabla de surf**
TAH-bla day SOORF

surgery (n)
la **cirugía**
see-roo-HEE-ah

surprise (n)
la **sorpresa**
sor-PRAY-sah

surprising (adj)
sorprendente
sor-pren-DEN-tay

swan (n)
el **cisne**
SISS-nay

sweater (n)
el **suéter**
SOO'EH-tair

swimming (n)
la **natación**
na-ta-SE'ON

swimming pool (n)
la **piscina**
piss-SEE-na

swimsuit (n)
el **traje de baño**
TRAH-Hay day BAH-n'yo

swing (n)
el **columpio**
ko-LOOM-pe'oh

symbol (n)
el **símbolo**
SEEM-bo-lo

T

tadpole
el renacuajo

table (n)
la **mesa**
MAY-sah

table tennis (n)
el **tenis de mesa**
TAY-niss day may-sa

tadpole (n)
el **renacuajo**
rray-nah-KOO'AH-Hoh

tail (n)
la **cola**
KOH-la

tall (adj)
alto (m)
AHL-to

tape measure (n)
la **cinta métrica**
SEEN-ta MAY-tree-ka

taxi (n)
el **taxi**
TAK-see

tea (n)
el **té**
TAY

taxi
el taxi

teacher (n)
el **maestro**
mah-ESS-tro
la **maestra**
mah-ESS-tra

team (n)
el **equipo**
ay-KEE-po

teddy bear (n)
el **osito de peluche**
o-SEE-to day pay-LOO-chay

telescope (n)
el **telescopio**
tay-less-KOH-pee'oh

television (n)
la **televisión**
tay-lay-be-SEE'ON

tennis (n)
el **tenis**
TAY-niss

tent (n)
la **tienda de campaña**
TEE'EN-da day kam-PA-n'ya

term (semester) (n)
el **término**
TAIR-mee-no

terrible (adj)
terrible
tay-RREE-blay

text message (n)
el **mensaje escrito**
men-SAH-Hay ess-KREE-to

that (adj)
ese (m) **esa** (f)
eh-say/eh-sah

A B C D E F G H I J K L M N O P Q R **S T** U V W X Y Z

tongue
la lengua

toad
el sapo

the (article)
el/la/los/las
ell/lah/los/las

their (adj)
su/sus
SOO/SOOS

then (conj)
después
dess-POO'ESS

there (adv)
allí (m) allá (f)
ah-L'YI/ah-L'YA

thermometer (n)
el termómetro
tair-MOH-may-tro

they (pron)
ellos (m) ellas (f)
EH-l'yos/EH-l'yas

thick (adj)
grueso (m)
GROO'EH-so

thin (adj)
delgado (m)
dell-GAH-do

thing (n)
la cosa
KOH-sa

third (adj)
tercero (m)
tair-SAY-ro

thirsty (adj)
sediento (m)
say-DEE'EN-to

this (adj)
este (m) esta (f)
ESS-tay/ESS-tah

thousand
mil/millar
MEEL/mee-L'YAR

through (prep)
a través
ah tra-BESS

thumb (n)
el pulgar
pool-GAR

thumbtack (n)
la chincheta
cheen-CHAY-tah

thunderstorm (n)
la tormenta
tor-MEN-tah

tick (n)
el boleto
boh-LAY-toh

ticket (n)
la entrada
en-TRAH-da

tide (n)
la marea
ma-RAY-ah

tie (n)
la corbata
kor-BAH-ta

tiger (n)
el tigre
TEE-gray

tight (adj)
apretado (m)
ah-pray-TAH-do

tights (n)
las medias
MAY-de'ahs

time (n)
el tiempo
TE'EM-poh

timetable (n)
el horario
o-RAH-re'oh

tiny (adj)
diminuto (m)
de-me-NOO-to

tire (n)
la llanta
L'YAHN-ta

tired (adj)
cansado (m)
kan-SAH-do

tissues (n)
los pañuelos de papel
pah-N'YU'AY-los day pah-PELL

toad (n)
el sapo
SAH-po

toaster (n)
la tostadora
toss-ta-DOR-ra

today (adv)
hoy
O'EE

toe (n)
el dedo del pie
DAY-do del PEE'EH

together (adv)
juntos (m) juntas (f)
HOON-tos/HOON-tas

toilet (n)
el inodoro
ee-no-DOH-ro

whiskers
los bigotes

tiger
el tigre

stripes
las rayas

tail
la cola

A B C D E F G H I J K L M N O P Q R S **T** U V W X Y Z

toothbrush
el cepillo de dientes

toilet paper (n)
el papel higiénico
pah-PELL ee-HAY-nee-ko

tomato (n)
el tomate
to-MAH-te

tomorrow (adv)
mañana
ma-N'YAH-na

tongue (n)
la lengua
LEN-goo'ah

tonight (adv)
esta noche
ESS-ta NO-chay

too (adv)
también
tam-BE'EN

tool (n)
la herramienta
air-rrah-MEE'EN-ta

tooth (n)
el diente
DEE'EN-tay

toothbrush (n)
el cepillo de
dientes
*say-PEE-l'yo day
DEE'EN-tess*

toothpaste (n)
la pasta de dientes
*PASS-ta day
DEE'EN-tess*

top (n)
la parte de arriba
*PAIR-tay day
ahr-RREE-ba*

torch (n)
la antorcha
ahn-TOHR-chah

tornado (n)
el tornado
tor-NAH-do

tortoise (n)
la tortuga
tohr-TOO-ga

toucan (n)
el tucán
too-KAN

tough (adj)
duro (m)
DOO-ro

tourist (n)
el turista
too-RISS-ta

toward (prep)
hacia
AH-se'ah

towel (n)
la toalla
to-AH-l'ya

town (n)
la ciudad
se'oo-DAHD

toy (n)
el juguete
Hoo-GAY-tay

toy box (n)
el baúl de los
juguetes
*bah-OOL day los
Hoo-GAY-tess*

tortoise
la tortuga

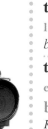
traffic lights
el semáforo

tractor (n)
el tractor
TRAK-tor

traffic (n)
el tráfico
TRAH-fee-ko

traffic lights (n)
el semáforo
say-MAH-for-ro

train (n)
el tren
TREN

train set (n)
el tren eléctrico
TREN ay-LEK-tree-ko

transport (n)
el transporte
trans-POHR-tay

trash (n)
la basura
bah-SOO-rah

trash can (n)
el cubo de la
basura
*KOO-bo deh lah
bah-SOO-rah*

tray (n)
la bandeja
ban-DAY-Hah

tree (n)
el árbol
AHR-bol

triangle (n)
el triángulo
tree-AHN-goo-lo

trip (n)
el viaje
BE'AH-Hay

tropical (adj)
tropical
tro-pe-KAHL

trouble (n)
el problema
pro-BLAY-ma

trowel (n)
el desplantador
dess-plahn-tah-DOR

truck (n)
el camión
ka-ME'ON

trunk
la trompa

90

turkey
el pavo

true (adj)
cierto (m)
SE'AIR-to

trunk (animal) (n)
la trompa
TROHM-pa

trunk (tree) (n)
el tronco
TROHN-ko

T-shirt (n)
la camiseta
ka-mee-SAY-ta

tube (n)
el tubo
TOO-bo

tunnel (n)
el túnel
TOO-nell

turkey (n)
el pavo
PAH-bo

turtle (n)
la tortuga (marina)
tohr-TOO-ga
(mah-REE-nah)

twice (adv)
dos veces
DOSS BAY-sess

twin (n)
el gemelo
Hay-MAY-lo

U

ugly (adj)
feo (m)
FAY-oh

umbrella (n)
el paraguas
pair-RAH-goo'ahs

uncle (n)
el tío
TEE-o

under (prep)
bajo
BAH-Ho

underground (adj)
subterráneo (m)
soob-tay-RRAH-nay-o

underwear (n)
la ropa interior
RRO-pa in-tay-RE'OR

unfair (adj)
injusto (m)
in-HOOS-to

uniform (n)
el uniforme
oo-nee-FOHR-may

universe (n)
el universo
oo-nee-BAIR-so

umbrella
el paraguas

handle
el mango

uniform
el uniforme

until (prep)
hasta
AHS-ta

unusual (adj)
extraño (m)
eks-trah-n'yo

upside down (adv)
al revés
ahl ray-BESS

upstairs (adv)
arriba
ah-RREE-ba

useful (adj)
útil
OO-teel

usually (adv)
normalmente
nor-mahl-MEN-tay

V

van (n)
la furgoneta
foor-go-NAY-ta

vegetable (n)
la verdura
bair-DOO-ra

vegetarian (n)
el vegetariano
bay-gay-tah-ree-AH-no
la vegetariana
bay-gay-tah-ree-AH-na

verb (n)
el verbo
BAIR-bo

very (adv)
muy
MOO'EE

vet (n)
el veterinario
bay-tair-ree-NAH-re'o
la veterinaria
bay-tair-ree-NAH-re'a

video (n)
el video
BEE-day-oh

video game (n)
el videojuego
BEE-day-oh-HOO'AY-go

village (n)
el pueblo
POO'AY-blo

violin (n)
el violín
be'o-LEEN

violin
el violín

A B C D E F G H I J K L M N O P Q R S **T U V** W X Y Z

W

watering can
la regadera

waist (n)
la cintura
seen-TOO-ra

waiter (n)
el camarero
ka-ma-RAY-ro

waitress (n)
la camarera
ka-ma-RAY-ra

walk (n)
el paseo
pa-SAY-o

wall (n)
la pared
pa-REHD

war (n)
la guerra
GAY-rrah

wardrobe (n)
el armario
ahr-MAH-re'o

warm (adj)
cálido (m)
KAH-le-do

warning (n)
la advertencia
ahd-bair-TEN-se'ah

washcloth (n)
el paño
PAH-n'yo

washing machine (n)
la lavadora
la-ba-DO-ra

wasp (n)
la avispa
ah-BEES-pa

watch (n)
el reloj
ray-lOH

water (n)
el agua
AH-goo'ah

water lily (n)
el nenúfar
nay-NOO-far

watering can (n)
la regadera
ray-ga-DAY-ra

watermelon (n)
la sandía
san-DEE-a

wave (n)
la ola
O-la

wax (n)
la cera
SAY-ra

wave
la ola

we (pron)
nosotros (m)
no-SOH-tros

nosotras (f)
no-SOH-tras

weak (adj)
débil
DAY-bil

weather (n)
el tiempo
TE'AYM-po

Web site (n)
el sitio web
SEE-te'o OO'EB

weed (n)
la mala hierba
MAH-la EE'AIR-ba

week (n)
la semana
say-MAH-na

weekend (n)
el fin de semana
FEEN-day say-MAH-na

welcome (adj)
bienvenido (m)
be'en-bay-NEE-do

well (adj)
bien
BE'EN

west (n)
el oeste
o-ESS-tay

wet (adj)
mojado (m)
mo-HAH-do

whale (n)
la ballena
ba-L'YAY-na

wheat (n)
el trigo
TREE-go

wheel (n)
la rueda
ROO'AY-da

wheelbarrow (n)
la carretilla
ka-rray-TEE-l'ya

wheelchair (n)
la silla de ruedas
SEE-l'yah day ROO'AY-das

when (adv)
cuando/cuándo
KOO'AHN-do

where (adv)
donde/dónde
DOHN-day

while (conj)
durante
doo-RAHN-tay

whisker (n)
el bigote
be-GO-tay

whistle (n)
el silbato
sil-BAH-to

white (adj)
blanco (m)
BLAHN-ko

who (pron)
quién/quiénes
KEE'EN/KEE'EH'nes

why (adv)
por qué
pohr KAY

wide (adj)
ancho (m)
AHN-cho

wing
el ala

wife (n)
la **esposa**
ess-POH-sa

wild (adj)
salvaje
sal-BA-Hay

wind (n)
el **viento**
BE'EN-to

windmill (n)
el **molino de viento**
mo-LEE-no day BE'EN-to

window (n)
la **ventana**
ben-TAH-na

windy (adj)
de **mucho viento**
day MOO-cho BE'EN-to

wing (n)
el **ala**
AH-la

winner (n)
el **ganador**
ga-na-DOHR

la **ganadora**
ga-na-DO-ra

winter (n)
el **invierno**
in-BE'AIR-no

with (prep)
con
KOHN

without (prep)
sin
SEEN

wolf (n)
el **lobo**
LOH-bo

woman (n)
la **mujer**
moo-HAIR

wood (n)
la **madera**
ma-DAY-ra

wooden (adj)
de **madera**
day ma-DAY-ra

wool (n)
la **lana**
lah-na

wool hat (n)
el **gorro de lana**
GO-rroh day LAH-na

word (n)
la **palabra**
pa-LAH-bra

world (n)
el **mundo**
MOON-do

worm (n)
el **gusano**
goo-SAH-no

worse (adj)
peor
pay-OHR

worst (adj)
el **peor**
pay-OHR

writing (n)
la **escritura**
ess-kree-TOO-ra

Y

yacht
el yate

yacht (n)
el **yate**
IA-tay

year (n)
el **año**
AH-n'yo

yellow (adj)
amarillo (m)
ah-mah-REE-l'yo

yesterday (adv)
ayer
ah-YAIR

yogurt (n)
el **yogur**
ee'oh-GOOR

you (pron)
tú
TOO

young (adj)
joven
HO-ben

your (pron)
tu
your

youth hostel (n)
el **albergue**
ahl-BAIR-gay

Z

zebra
la cebra

zebra (n)
la **cebra**
SAY-bra

zip code (n)
el **código postal**
KOH-de-go pos-'TAHL

zipper (n)
la **cremallera**
kray-ma-L'YAY-ra

zone (n)
la **zona**
SOH-na

zoo (n)
el **zoo**
SO'OH

zipper
la cremallera

A B C D E F G H I J K L M N O P Q R S T U V **W** X **Y Z**

93

Spanish A–Z

In this section, Spanish words are in alphabetical order. They are followed by the English translation and a few letters to indicate what type of word it is – a noun (n) or adjective (adj), for example. Look at p56 to see a list of the different types of words.

Nouns in Spanish are either masculine or feminine. We have used (m) and (f) to tell you which they are. Sometimes a word in Spanish might mean more than one thing in English, so there might be two translations underneath.

Most of the nouns (naming words) here describe just one thing, so they are singular. To make a noun plural (for more than one thing) you usually just add an "s" – the same as in English. In Spanish though, the other words in the sentence change too – *el* becomes *los* and *la* becomes *las*. The adjectives also change, usually getting an extra "s" at the end. In Spanish, an adjective usually comes after the noun too.

A

a él/para él (pron)
him

a ella/para ella (pron)
her

a menudo (adv)
often

a mí (pron)
me

a través (prep)
through

a través de (prep)
across

a veces (adv)
sometimes

abajo (prep)
below

abecedario (n) (m)
alphabet

abeja (n) (f)
bee

abierto (adj)
open

abrigo (n) (m)
coat

abuela (n) (f)
grandmother

abuelo (n) (m)
grandfather

abuelos (n) (m, plu)
grandparents

aburrido (adj)
boring

acampada (n) (f)
camping

acantilado (n) (m)
cliff

accidente (n) (m)
accident

aceite (n) (m)
oil

acerca de (prep)
about

actividad (n) (f)
activity

adelante (adv)
forward

adentro (prep)
into

adicional (adj)
extra

adulto (adj)
adult

advertencia (n) (f)
warning

afilado (adj)
sharp

afortunado (adj)
lucky

afuera (adv)
outside

agenda (n) (m)
calendar

agua (n) (m)
water

aguacate (n) (m)
avocado

águila (n) (m)
eagle

aguja (n) (f)
needle

agujero (n) (m)
hole

ahora (adv)
now

ajedrez (n) (m)
chess

al revés (adv)
upside down; backward

ala (n) (m)
wing

ala delta (n) (f)
hang-glider

alacena (n) (f)
cupboard

aleta (n) (f)
fin; flipper

alfabeto (n) (m)
alphabet

alfombra (n) (f)
carpet

alfombrilla del ratón (n) (f)
mouse pad

algas (n) (f, plu)
seaweed

algo (pron)
something

algodón (n) (m)
cotton

alguien (pron)
someone

algunos (adj)
some

allí/allá (adv)
over there, there

almohada (n) (f)
pillow

almuerzo (n) (m)
lunch

alrededor (adv)
around

alrededor (prep)
about

alto (adj)
loud; tall; high

alumno/alumna (n) (m/f)
student

amable (adj)
kind; gentle

amarillo (adj)
yellow

ambulancia (n) (f)
ambulance

amigable (adj)
friendly

amigo/amiga (n) (m/f)
friend

anaranjado (adj)
orange

ancho (adj)
wide

anciano/anciana (n) (m/f)
old person

ancla (n) (m)
anchor

anillo (n) (m)
ring

animal (n) (m)
animal

antena (n) (f)
antenna

antes (prep)
before

antorcha (n) (f)
torch

apariencia (n) (f)
appearance

apartamento (n) (m)
apartment

aparte (adv)
apart

apretado (adj)
tight

araña (n) (f)
spider

árbol (n) (m)
tree

arbusto (n) (m)
bush

arco (n) (m)
arch

arcoiris (n) (m)
rainbow

ardilla (n) (f)
squirrel

área (n) (m)
area

arena (n) (f)
sand

arete (n) (m)
earring

armario (n) (m)
wardrobe

arriba (adv)
upstairs

arroz (n) (m)
rice

arte (n) (m)
art

artista (n) (m/f)
artist

ascensor (n) (m)
elevator

asistente (n) (m/f)
assistant

asombroso (adj)
amazing

astronauta (n) (m/f)
astronaut

astrónomo/astrónoma (n) (m/f)
astronomer

asustado (adj)
frightened

atardecer (n) (m)
sunset

aterrador (adj)
frightening

ático (n) (m)
attic

atlas (n) (m)
atlas

atletismo (n) (m)
athletics

auto (n) (m)
car

autobús (n) (m)
bus

autopista (n) (f)
highway

aventura (n) (f)
adventure

avión (n) (m)
airplane; jet

avispa (n) (f)
wasp

¡Ay!
Ouch!

ayuda (n) (f)
help

azúcar (n) (m)
sugar

azul (adj)
blue

B

babuino (n) (m)
baboon

bádminton (n) (m)
badminton

bailarín/bailarina (n) (m/f)
dancer; ballet dancer

bajo (adj)
low; short

bajo (prep)
under

balcón (n) (m)
balcony

ballena (n) (f)
whale

balón de fútbol (n) (m)
soccer ball

banco (n) (m)
bench; bank (for money)

banda (n) (f)
band

bandeja (n) (f)
tray

bandera (n) (f)
flag

baño (n) (m)
bathroom; bath

barato (adj)
cheap

barba (n) (f)
beard

barbacoa (n) (f)
barbecue

barbilla (n) (f)
chin

barco (n) (m)
ship; boat

barco de pesca (n) (m)
fishing boat

barrio (n) (m)
neighborhood

barro (n) (m)
mud

básquetbol (n) (m)
basketball

basura (n) (f)
trash

batalla (n) (f)
battle

bate (n) (m)
bat (for sport)

batería (n) (f)
drum kit

batido (n) (m)
milk shake

baúl (n) (m)
chest

baúl de los juguetes (n)(m)
toy box

bebé (n) (m)
baby

bebida (n) (f)
drink

béisbol (n) (m)
baseball

belleza (n) (f)
beauty

beso (n) (m)
kiss

biblioteca (n) (f)
library

bicicleta (n) (f)
bike

bicicleta de montaña (n)(f)
mountain bike

bien (adv)
well; fine

bienvenido (adj)
welcome

bigote (n) (m)
moustache; whisker
(of animal)

billón
billion

binoculares (n) (f)
binoculars

blanco (adj)
white

blando (adj)
soft

blusa (n) (f)
blouse

boca (n) (f)
mouth

bocina (n) (f)
horn (of vehicle)

bola (n) (f)
ball

bola de nieve (n) (f)
snowball

boleto (n) (m)
ticket

bolsa (n)
pouch; bag

bolsa de la compra (n) (f)
shopping bag

bolsa de la escuela (n) (f)
school bag

bolsa de plástico (n) (f)
plastic bag

bolsillo (n) (m)
pocket

bolso (n) (m)
purse; handbag

bombero/bombera (n) (m/f)
firefighter

bombilla (n) (f)
light bulb

bonito (adj)
nice; pretty, beautiful

bosque (n) (m)
forest

bota (n) (f)
boot

bote (n) (m)
boat

bote de remos (n) (m)
rowboat

bote salvavidas (n) (m)
lifeboat

botella (n) (f)
bottle

botón (n) (m)
button

boya (n) (f)
buoy

brazo (n) (m)
arm

brillante (adj)
shiny; brilliant

brisa (n) (f)
breeze

brújula (n) (f)
compass

bueno (adj)
good

bufanda (n) (f)
scarf

búho (n) (m)
owl

bulbo (n) (m)
bulb (of plant)

burbuja (n) (f)
bubble

buzón (n) (m)
mailbox

C

caballero (n) (m)
knight

caballo (n) (m)
horse

cabeza (n) (f)
head

cabra (n) (f)
goat

cacahuate (n) (m)
peanut

cada (adj)
each; every

cadena (n) (f)
chain

cadera (n) (f)
hip

café (adj)
brown

café (n) (m)
coffee; café

caimán (n) (m)
alligator

caja (n) (f)
box; checkout

caja de cerillas (n) (f)
matchbox

caja registradora (n) (f)
cash register

cajón (n) (m)
drawer

calabaza (n) (f)
pumpkin

calcetín (n) (m)
sock

calculadora (n) (f)
calculator

calendario (n) (m)
calendar

cálido (adj)
warm

caliente (adj)
hot

calle (n) (f)
street

calmado (adj)
calm

calor (n) (m)
heat

cama (n) (f)
bed

cámara (n) (f)
camera

camarero/camarera (n) (m/f)
waiter/waitress

cambio (n) (m)
change

camello (n) (m)
camel

camino (n) (m)
road, route

camión (n) (m)
truck

camisa (n) (f)
shirt

camiseta (n) (f)
T-shirt

campana (n) (f)
bell

campo (n) (m)
countryside; field

cangrejo (n) (m)
crab

canguro (n) (m)
kangaroo

canica (n) (f)
marble (toy)

canoa (n) (f)
canoe

cansado (adj)
tired

capa (n) (f)
layer; cloak

caparazón (n) (m)
shell

capital (n) (f)
capital

capucha (n) (f)
hood

cara (n) (f)
face

caracol (n) (m)
snail

caramelo (n) (m)
candy

carne (n)
meat; flesh

caro (adj)
expensive

carrera (n) (f)
race

carretilla (n) (f)
wheelbarrow (n)

carrito de compras (n) (m)
shopping cart

carro (n) (m)
cart

carta (n) (f)
letter; card; menu

cartel (n) (m)
poster

cartero/cartera (n) (m/f)
mail carrier

cartón (n) (m)
cardboard

casa (n) (f)
house; home

casado (adj)
married

casco (n) (m)
helmet

casi (adv)
nearly; almost

castillo de arena (n) (m)
sandcastle

cazo (n) (m)
saucepan

cebolla (n) (f)
onion

cebra (n) (f)
zebra

ceja (n) (f)
eyebrow

cena (n) (f)
dinner

centro (n) (m)
center

cepillo de dientes (n) (m)
toothbrush

cepillo de pelo (n) (m)
hairbrush

cera (n) (f)
wax

cerca (adv)
near

cerca (n) (f)
fence

cercano (adj)
close

cerdo (n) (m)
pig

cereal (n) (m)
cereal

cerebro (n) (m)
brain

cerilla (n) (m)
match

cerrado (adj)
closed

césped (n) (m)
lawn

ccsta (n) (f)
basket

chaleco (n) (m)
vest

chaleco salvavidas (n) (m)
life jacket

champú (n) (m)
shampoo

chaqueta (n) (f)
jacket

chef (n) (m/f)
chef

chicle (n) (m)
chewing gum

chico/chica (n) (m/f)
boy/girl

chimenea (n) (f)
chimney

chimpancé (n) (m)
chimpanzee

chincheta (n) (f)
thumbtack

chiste (n) (m)
joke

chocolate (n) (m)
chocolate

chocolate caliente (n) (m)
hot chocolate

chubasquero (n) (m)
raincoat

ciclismo (n) (m)
cycling

cielo (n) (m)
sky

ciencias (n) (f)
science

científico/científica (n) (m/f)
scientist

cierto (adj)
true

ciervo (n) (m)
deer

cine (n) (m)
cinema

cinta (n)
ribbon; cassette

cinta métrica (n) (f)
tape measure

cintura (n) (f)
waist

cinturón (n) (m)
belt

circo (n) (m)
circus

círculo (n) (m)
circle

cirugía (n) (f)
surgery

cisne (n) (m)
swan

cita (n) (f)
date

ciudad (n) (f)
town; city

claro (adj)
light, pale (in color); clear

clavícula (n) (f)
collar bone

cliente/clienta (n) (m/f)
customer; shopper

coche de bomberos (n) (m)
fire engine

coche de carreras (n) (m)
racing car

coche de policía (n) (m)
police car

cocina (n) (f)
stove; kitchen

coco (n) (m)
coconut

cocodrilo (n) (m)
crocodile

código postal (n) (m)
zip code

codo (n) (m)
elbow

cohete (espacial) (n) (m)
(space) rocket

cojín (n) (m)
cushion

col (n) (f)
cabbage

cola (n) (f)
line; glue; tail (of animal)

colibrí (n) (m)
hummingbird

colina (n) (f)
hill

collar (n) (m)
necklace; collar

colmena (n) (f)
hive

color (n) (m)
color

colorido (adj)
colorful

columpio (n) (m)
swing

comedor (n) (m)
dining room

cometa (n) (f)
kite

comida (n) (f)
food

cómo (adv)
how

como (prep)
like

cómoda (n) (f)
chest of drawers

cómodo (adj)
comfortable

compañero/compañera (n) (m/f)
partner

computadora (n) (f)
computer

computadora portátil (n) (f)
laptop

con (prep)
with

concha (n) (f)
shell

concierto (n) (m)
concert

concurso (n) (m)
contest

conejillo de indias (n) (m)
guinea pig

conejo (n) (m)
rabbit

congelador (n) (m)
freezer

continente (n) (m)
continent

copo de nieve (n) (m)
snowflake

corazón (n) (m)
heart

corbata (n) (f)
tie

cordero (n) (m)
lamb

corona (n) (f)
crown

correcto (adj)
right; correct

correo (n) (m)
mail

correo electrónico (n) (m)
email

cortacésped (n) (m)
lawn mower

cortina (n) (f)
curtain

corto (adj)
short

cosa (n) (f)
thing

cosecha (n) (f)
crop; harvest

cosechadora combinada (n) (f)
combine harvester

costa (n) (f)
coast; shore

costilla (n) (f)
rib

crema (n) (f)
cream

cremallera (n) (f)
zipper

creyón (n) (m)
crayon

criatura (n) (f)
creature

cruce (n) (m)
crossing

cuadrado (n) (m)
square

cualquier/cualquiera (pron)
anybody; anything

cuando/cuándo (adv)
when

cuarto (n) (m)
quarter; room

cuarto de los niños (n) (m)
nursery

cubierta (n) (f)
deck

cubo (n) (m)
bucket; cube

cubo de la basura (n) (m)
trash can

cuchara (n) (f)
spoon

cuchillo (n) (m)
knife

cuello (n) (m)
collar; neck

cuenta (n) (f)
bill; bead

cuento (n) (m)
story

cuerda (n) (f)
rope; string

cuerda de saltar (n) (f)
jump rope

cuerno (n) (m)
horn (of animal)

cuero (n) (m)
leather

cuerpo (n) (m)
body

cueva (n) (f)
cave

cuidadoso (adj)
careful

cumbre (n) (f)
summit

cumpleaños (n) (m)
birthday

cúpula (n) (f)
dome

curioso (adj)
curious

curso (n) (m)
term, semester

curvado (adj)
curved

D

dados (n) (m)
dice

de madera (adj)
wooden

de/desde (prep)
from

de moda (adj)
fashionable

de mucho viento (adj)
windy

de nuevo (adv)
again

de repente (adv)
suddenly

de verdad (adv)
really

debajo (prep)
below; under

débil (adj)
weak

decoración (n) (f)
decoration

dedo (n) (m)
finger

dedo del pie (n) (m)
toe

delantal (n) (m)
apron

delfín (n) (m)
dolphin

delgado (adj)
thin

delicioso (adj)
delicious

demasiado (adv)
too

dentista (n) (m/f)
dentist

dentro (prep)
into; inside

deporte (n) (m)
sport

deprisa (adv)
quickly

derecha (n) (f)
right (side)

desafío (n) (m)
challenge

desayuno (n) (m)
breakfast

descubrimiento (n) (m)
discovery

desfile (n) (m)
parade

desierto (n) (m)
desert

despacio (adv)
slowly

despertador (n) (m)
alarm clock

desplantador (n) (m)
trowel

después (conj)
then

después (de) (prep)
past; after

detrás (prep)
behind

día (n) (m)
day

diagrama (n) (m)
diagram

diamante (n) (m)
diamond

dibujo (n) (m)
picture; drawing

diccionario (n) (m)
dictionary

diente (n) (m)
tooth

diferente (adj)
different

difícil (adj)
difficult

digital (adj)
digital

diminuto (adj)
tiny

dinero (n) (m)
money

dinero en efectivo (n) (m)
cash

dinosaurio (n) (m)
dinosaur

dirección (n) (f)
address; direction

dirección de correo electrónico (n) (f)
email address

directamente (adv)
directly

disco (n) (f)
disco

disco compacto (n) (m)
CD

disco duro (n) (m)
hard drive

discurso (n) (m)
speech

disfraz (n) (m)
costume

distancia (n) (f)
distance

divertido (adj)
fun

divorciado (adj)
divorced

doctor/doctora (n) (m/f)
doctor

dolor de cabeza (n) (m)
headache

dolor de oído (n) (m)
earache

donde/dónde (adv)
where

dormitorio (n) (m)
bedroom

dos veces (adv)
twice

dragón (n) (m)
dragon

ducha (n) (f)
shower

durante (prep/conj)
during, while

duro (adj)
tough; hard

E

e (conj)
and (before i/hi)

eco (n) (m)
echo

ecuador (n) (m)
equator

edificio (n) (m)
building

edredón (n) (m)
comforter

efecto (n) (m)
effect

ejercicio (n) (m)
exercise

ejército (n) (m)
army

el (article) (m, sing)
the

él (pron)
he

elástico (n) (m)
rubber band

eléctrico (adj)
electrical

elefante (n) (m)
elephant

ella (pron)
she

ello (pron)
it

ellos/ellas (pron) (m/f, plu)
they

emergencia (n) (f)
emergency

emocionado (adj)
excited

empate (n) (m)
tie

empinado (adj)
steep

en primer lugar (adv)
first

encantador (adj)
lovely

enchufe (n) (m)
plug

enciclopedia (n) (f)
encyclopedia

encima de (prep)
on top of

enfadado (adj)
angry

enfangado (adj)
muddy

enfermedad (n) (f)
illness

enfermero/enfermera (n) (m/f)
nurse

enfermo (adj)
sick, ill

enorme (adj)
huge

ensalada (n) (f)
salad

entonces (conj)
then

entrada (n) (f)
entrance

entre (prep)
between

entrenador/entrenadora (n) (m/f)
coach

entusiasta (adj)
enthusiastic

equipaje (n) (m)
luggage

equipo (n) (m)
team; equipment

error (n) (m)
mistake

escalera (n) (f)
ladder; stairs

escalón (n) (m)
step

escarabajo (n) (m)
beetle

escoba (n) (f)
broom

escondidas (n) (f)
hide-and-seek

escritorio (n) (m)
desk

escritura (n) (f)
writing

escuela (n) (f)
school

ese/esa (adj)
that

ése/ésa (pron)
that one

espacio (n) (m)
space

espaguetis (n) (m)
spaghetti

espalda (n) (f)
back (body)

español (n) (m)
Spanish

espantoso (adj)
frightening

especial (adj)
special

espectáculo (n) (m)
show

espectáculo de marionetas (n) (m)
puppet show

espejo (n) (m)
mirror

esponja (n) (f)
sponge

esposo/esposa (n) (m/f)
husband/wife

esqueleto (n) (m)
skeleton

esquí (n) (m)
ski

esquina (n) (f)
corner

esta noche (adv)
tonight

estación (n) (f)
station; season

estación de tren (n) (f)
railway station

estampado (n) (m)
pattern

estanque (n) (m)
pond

estante (n) (m)
shelf

estatua (n) (f)
statue

este (n) (m)
east

este/esta (adj)
this

éste/ésta (pron)
this one

estómago (n) (m)
stomach

estrecho (adj)
narrow

estrella (n) (f)
star

estrella de mar (n) (f)
starfish

estricto (adj)
strict

estudiante (n) (m/f)
student

estúpido (adj)
stupid

evento (n) (m)
event

exacto (adv)
just

examen (n) (m)
exam

excelente (adj)
excellent

expedición (n) (f)
expedition

experimento (n) (m)
experiment

experto (n) (m)
expert

explorador (n) (m)
explorer

explosión (n) (f)
explosion

extinto (adj)
extinct

extraño (adj)
strange; unusual; foreign

extremadamente (adv)
extremely

F

fábrica (n) (f)
factory

fabuloso (adj)
fabulous

fácil (adj)
easy

factura (n) (f)
bill

falda (n) (f)
skirt

falso (adj)
false

familia (n) (f)
family

famoso (adj)
famous

fantástico (adj)
fantastic

**farmacéutico/
farmacéutica (n) (m/f)**
pharmacist

faro (n) (m)
lighthouse

favorito (adj)
favorite

feliz (adj)
happy

felpudo (n) (m)
mat

fémur (n) (m)
thigh bone

feo (adj)
ugly

feria (n) (f)
fair

festival (n) (m)
festival

fideo (n) (m)
noodle

fieltro (n) (m)
felt

fiesta (n) (f)
party

figura (n) (f)
shape

filo (n) (m)
edge

fin (n) (m)
end

fin de semana (n) (m)
weekend

final (n) (m)
end

fino (adj)
thin

flauta (n) (f)
flute

flecha (n) (f)
arrow

flor (n) (f)
flower

foca (n) (f)
seal

fondo (n) (m)
bottom

forma (n) (f)
shape

forro polar (n) (m)
fleece (clothing)

fósil (n) (m)
fossil

foto (n) (f)
photo

frambuesa (n) (f)
raspberry

frase (n) (f)
phrase

fregadero (n) (m)
sink (in kitchen)

fresa (n) (f)
strawberry

fresco (adj)
cool; fresh

frijoles (n) (m)
beans

frío (adj)
cold

fruta (n) (f)
fruit

fuego (n) (m)
fire

fuera (adv)
outside

fuera de (prep)
out of

fuerte (adj)
strong

furgoneta (n) (f)
van

fútbol (n) (m)
soccer (game)

fútbol americano (n) (m)
football (game)

futuro (n) (m)
future

G

gafas (n) (f)
glasses

gafas de agua (n) (f)
goggles

gafas de sol (n) (f)
sunglasses

galleta (n) (f)
cookie

**ganador/ganadora
(n) (m/f)**
winner

garaje (n) (m)
garage

garra (n) (f)
claw; paw

garrapata (n) (f)
tick

garza (n) (f)
heron

gasolina (n) (f)
gasoline

gatito (n) (m)
kitten

gato (n) (m)
cat

gaviota (n) (m)
seagull

gemelo/gemela (n) (m/f)
twin

gente (n) (f)
people

gigante (n) (m)
giant

gimnasia (n) (f)
gymnastics

girasol (n) (m)
sunflower

giro (n) (m)
turn

glaciar (n) (m)
glacier

globo (n) (m)
balloon

globo aerostático (n) (m)
hot air balloon

globo terráqueo (n) (m)
globe

gobierno (n) (m)
government

gol (n) (m)
goal

golf (n) (m)
golf

goma (n) (f)
eraser

gordo (adj)
fat

gorila (n) (m)
gorilla

gorra (n) (f)
cap

gorro de lana (n) (m)
wool hat

gota (n) (f)
drop

gran/grande (adj)
big; great

granero (n) (m)
barn

granja (n) (f)
farm

granjero/granjera (n) (m/f)
farmer

grifo (n) (m)
faucet

grúa (n) (f)
crane

grueso (adj)
thick

grulla (n) (f)
crane

grupo (n) (m)
group

guante (n) (m)
glove

guerra (n) (f)
war

guía (n) (f)
guide

guijarro (n) (m)
pebble

guisante (n) (m)
pea

guitarra (n) (f)
guitar

gusano (n) (m)
earthworm

H

hábitat (n) (m)
habitat

hacia (prep)
toward

hacia atrás (adv)
backward

halcón (n) (m)
hawk

hambriento (adj)
hungry

hámster (n) (m)
hamster

harina (n) (f)
flour

hasta (adv)
even

hasta (prep)
until

hecho (n) (m)
fact

helado (n) (m)
ice cream

helecho (n) (m)
fern

helicóptero (n) (m)
helicopter

helicóptero de la policía (n) (m)
police helicopter

hembra (n) (f)
female

heno (n) (m)
hay

hermano/hermana (n) (m/f)
brother/sister

hermoso (adj)
hay

héroe/heroína (n) (m/f)
hero

herramienta (n) (f)
tool

hervidor (n) (m)
kettle

hielo (n) (m)
ice

hierba (n) (f)
grass

hijo/hija (n) (m/f)
son/daughter

hilo de pescar (n) (m)
fishing line

historia (n) (f)
history

histórico (adj)
historical

historieta (n) (f)
comic

hockey (n) (m)
hockey

hockey sobre hielo (n) (m)
ice hockey

hogar (n) (m)
home

hoja (n) (f)
leaf; sheet (of paper)

hola
hi

hombre (n) (m)
man

hombro (n) (m)
shoulder

hongo (n) (m)
mushroom

hora (n) (f)
hour

horario (n) (m)
timetable; schedule

horario (de una tienda) (n) (m)
opening hours

hormiga (n) (f)
ant

horno (n) (m)
oven

horrible (adj)
horrible

hospital (n) (m)
hospital

hotel (n) (m)
hotel

hoy (adv)
today

hueso (n) (m)
bone

huevo (n) (m)
egg

humano (n) (m)
human

humo (n) (m)
smoke

huracán (n) (m)
hurricane

I

idea (n) (f)
idea

idioma (n) (m)
language

igual (adj)
equal

imán (n) (m)
magnet

importante (adj)
important

imposible (adj)
impossible

incluso (adv)
even

información (n) (f)
information

informe (n) (m)
report

inglés (n) (m)
English

injusto (adj)
unfair

inmediatamente (adv)
immediately

inodoro (n) (m)
toilet

insecto (n) (m)
insect

insignia (n) (f)
badge

instrucción (n) (f)
instruction

instrumento (n) (m)
instrument

inteligente (adj)
smart

interesante (adj)
interesting

internacional (adj)
international

Internet (n) (f)
Internet

inundación (n) (f)
flood

invernadero (n) (m)
greenhouse

invierno (n) (m)
winter

invitación (n) (f)
invitation

isla (n) (f)
island

izquierda (n) (f)
left (side)

J

jabón (n) (m)
soap

jardín (n) (m)
garden

jardinería (n) (f)
gardening

jardinero/jardinera (n) (m/f)
gardener

jarra (n) (f)
jug

jaula (n) (f)
cage

jirafa (n) (f)
giraffe

joya (n) (f)
jewel

joyería (n) (f)
jewelry

judo (n) (m)
judo

juego (n) (m)
play; game

juego de tablero (n) (m)
board game

Juegos Olímpicos (n) (m)
Olympic Games

jugador/jugadora (n)(m/f)
player

jugo (n) (m)
juice

jugo de naranja (n) (m)
orange juice

juguete (n) (m)
toy

jungla (n) (m)
jungle

juntos/juntas (adv) (m/f)
together

K

karate (n) (m)
karate

koala (n) (m)
koala

L

la (article) (f, sing)
the

lagarto (n) (m)
lizard

lago (n) (m)
lake

lámpara (n) (f)
lamp

lana (n) (f)
wool

langosta (n) (f)
lobster

lápiz (n) (m)
pencil

lápiz de color (n) (m)
colored pencil

lápiz de labios (n) (m)
lipstick

largo (adj)
long

las (article) (f, plu)
the

lata (n) (f)
can

lata de pintura (n) (f)
paint can

lavabo (n) (m)
sink (in bathroom)

lavadora (n) (f)
washing machine

lazo (n) (m)
loop

lección (n) (f)
lesson

leche (n) (f)
milk

lechuga (n) (f)
lettuce

lectura (n) (f)
reading

lejos (adv)
far; away

lengua (n) (f)
tongue

lento (adj)
slow

león (n) (m)
lion

león marino (n) (m)
sea lion

leopardo (n)
leopard

lesión (n) (f)
injury

letra (n) (f)
letter (or alphabet)

ley (n) (f)
law

libélula (n) (f)
dragonfly

librería (n) (f)
bookstore

libreta (n) (f)
notebook

libro (n) (m)
book

ligero (adj)
light (in weight)

limón (n) (m)
lemon

limonada (n) (f)
lemonade

limpio (adj)
clean

línea (n) (f)
line

lío (n) (m)
mess

líquido (n) (m)
liquid

liso (adj)
smooth, flat

lista (n) (f)
list

lista de la compra (n) (f)
shopping list

listo (adj)
ready; clever

llanta (n) (f)
tire

llave (n) (f)
key

lleno (adj)
full

lleno de gente (adj)
crowded

lluvia (n) (f)
rain

lo (pron)
it

lobo (n) (m)
wolf

lonchera (n) (f)
lunchbox

loro (n) (m)
parrot

los (article) (m, plu)
the

luego (conj)
then

lugar (n) (m)
place

luna (n) (f)
moon

lupa (n) (f)
magnifying glass

luz (n) (f)
light

luz del sol (n) (f)
sunlight

M

madera (n) (f)
wood

madrastra (n) (f)
stepmother

madre (n) (f)
mother

maduro (adj)
ripe

maestro/maestra (n) (m/f)
teacher

magnético (adj)
magnetic

mago (n) (m)
magician

mala hierba (n) (f)
weed

maleta (n) (f)
suitcase

malo (adj)
bad

mamá (n) (f)
mom

mamífero (n) (m)
mammal

mañana (adv)
tomorrow

mañana (n) (f)
morning

mancha (n) (f)
spot

mando a distancia (n) (m)
remote control

mandos (n) (m)
controls

manga (n) (f)
sleeve

mano (n) (f)
hand

manopla (n) (f)
mitten; oven mitt

manta (n) (f)
blanket

mantequilla (n) (f)
butter

manzana (n) (f)
apple

mapa (n) (m)
map

maquillaje (n) (m)
make-up

máquina (n) (f)
machine

mar (n) (m)
sea

marca (n) (f)
mark

marcador (n) (m)
marker

marco (n) (m)
frame

marea (n) (f)
tide

margarita (n) (f)
daisy

marinero/marinera (n) (m/f)
sailor

marioneta (n) (f)
puppet

mariposa (n) (f)
butterfly

mariquita (n) (m)
ladybug

marisco (n) (m)
seafood

más de/más que (adj)
more than

máscara (n) (f)
mask

mascota (n) (f)
pet

matemáticas (n) (f)
math

materia (n) (f)
subject

mayúscula (n) (f)
capital

me (pron)
me

media (n) (f)
stocking

medianoche (n) (f)
midnight

medias (n) (f)
tights

medicina (n) (f)
medicine

medida (n) (f)
measurement

medio (n) (m)
middle

medio ambiente (n) (m)
environment

medusa (n) (f)
jellyfish

mejor (adj)
better

mejor (pron)
best

melón (n) (m)
melon

mensaje (n) (m)
message

mensaje escrito (n) (m)
text message

menú (n) (m)
menu

mercado (n) (m)
market

mermelada (n) (f)
jam

mes (n) (m)
month

mesa (n) (f)
table

metal (n) (m)
metal

metro (n) (m)
subway

mezcla (n) (f)
mixture

mi/mis (adj) (sing/plu)
my

microondas (n) (m)
microwave

miel (n) (f)
honey

mientras (conj)
while

mil/millar
thousand

millón
million

mineral (n) (m)
mineral

minusválido (adj)
disabled

minuto (n) (m)
minute (of time)

mismo (adj)
same

mitad (n) (f)
half

mochila (n) (f)
backpack

moda (n) (f)
fashion

mojado (adj)
wet

molino de viento (n) (m)
windmill

moneda (n) (f)
coin

mono (n) (m)
monkey

monopatín (n) (m)
skateboard

monstruo (n) (m)
monster

montaña (n) (f)
mountain

mosca (n) (f)
fly

motocicleta (n) (f)
motorcycle

motor (n) (m)
motor

mucho (adj)
(a) lot

muebles (n) (m)
furniture

muerto (adj)
dead

mujer (n) (f)
woman

multa (n) (f)
ticket

mundo (n) (m)
world

muñeca (n) (f)
doll

muñeco de nieve (n) (m)
snowman

murciélago (n) (m)
bat (animal)

museo (n) (m)
museum

música (n) (f)
music

músico/música (n) (m/f)
musician

muy (adv)
very

N

nacional (adj)
national

nada (pron)
nothing

nadie (pron)
nobody

naranja (n) (f)
orange (fruit)

nariz (n) (f)
nose

natación (n) (f)
swimming

naturaleza (n) (f)
nature

negocio (n) (m)
business

negro (adj)
black

nenúfar (n) (m)
water lily

nido (n) (m)
nest

niebla (n) (f)
fog

nieve (n) (f)
snow

ninguna parte (adv)
nowhere

niño (n) (m)
boy

niño/niña (n) (m/f)
child

niños/niñas (n) (m/f)
children (n)

noche (n) (f)
night; evening

nombre (n) (m)
name

normalmente (adv)
usually

norte (n) (m)
north

nosotros/nosotras (pron) (m/f, plu)
we

nota (n) (f)
note

noticia/noticias (n) (f, sing/plu)
news

novio (n) (m)
boyfriend

novia (n) (f)
girlfriend

nube (n) (f)
cloud

nublado (adj)
cloudy

nuestro/nuestra (adj) (m/f, sing)
our

nuestros/nuestras (adj) (m/f, pu)
our

nuevo (adj)
new

nudo (n) (m)
knot

número (n) (m)
number

nunca (adv)
never

O

o (conj)
or

objeto (n) (m)
object

océano (n) (m)
ocean

ocupado (adj)
busy

oeste (n) (m)
west

oficina (n) (f)
office

oficina de correos (n) (f)
post office

oído (n) (m)
ear

ojo (n) (m)
eye

ola (n) (f)
wave

óleo (n) (m)
oil

olor (n) (m)
smell

operación (n) (f)
operation

opuesto (adj)
opposite

oreja (n) (f)
ear

orilla (del río) (n) (f)
bank (of river)

orilla del mar (n) (f)
seaside

oro (n) (m)
gold

orquesta (n) (f)
orchestra

oruga (n) (f)
caterpillar

oscuro (adj)
dark

osito de peluche (n) (m)
teddy bear

oso (n) (m)
bear

oso polar (n) (m)
polar bear

otoño (n) (m)
fall (season)

otra vez (adv)
again

otro (adj)
other

óvalo (n) (m)
oval

oveja (n) (f)
sheep

P

pacient (adj)
patient

padrastro (n) (m)
stepfather

padre (n) (m)
parent; father

página (n) (f)
page

país (n) (m)
country

paja (n) (f)
straw

pajarito (n) (m)
chick

pájaro (n) (m)
bird

pajita (n) (f)
drinking straw

pala (n) (f)
shovel, spade

palabra (n) (f)
word

paleta (n) (f)
ice pop

pálido (adj)
faint, pale

palmera (n) (f)
palm tree

palo (n) (m)
stick, pole

pamela (n) (f)
sunhat

pan (n) (m)
bread

panadería (n) (f)
bakery

panda (n) (m)
panda

panecillo (n) (m)
roll

panqueque (n) (m)
pancake

paño (n) (m)
washcloth

paño de cocina (n) (m)
dish towel

pantalla (n) (f)
screen

pantalones (n) (m)
pants

pantalones cortos (n) (m)
shorts

pañuelo (n) (m)
handkerchief

pañuelos de papel (n) (m)
tissues

panza (n) (m)
stomach

papá (n) (m)
dad

papa (n) (f)
potato

papas fritas (n) (f)
French fries

papel (n) (m)
paper

papel higiénico (n) (m)
toilet paper

parada del autobús (n) (f)
bus stop

paraguas (n) (m)
umbrella

parasol (n) (m)
umbrella (for sun shade)

pared (n) (f)
wall

pareja (n) (f)
pair

parque (n) (m)
park

parque infantil (n) (m)
playground

parte (n) (f)
part

parte de arriba (n) (f)
top

parte de atrás (adj)
back

partido (n) (m)
match, game

pasado (n) (m)
past

pasajero/pasajera (n) (m/f)
passenger

pasaporte (n) (m)
passport

pasatiempo (n) (m)
hobby

paseo (n) (m)
walk

paso (n) (m)
step

pasta (n) (f)
pasta

pasta de dientes (n) (f)
toothpaste

pastel (n) (m)
cake

pata (n) (m)
paw; leg; foot (of animal or thing)

patínaje (sobre hielo/ en línea) (n) (m)
(ice/inline) skating

patito (n) (m)
duckling

pato (n) (m)
duck

patrón (n) (m)
pattern

pavimento (n) (m)
sidewalk

pavo (n) (m)
turkey

payaso/payasa (n) (m/f)
clown

paz (n) (f)
peace

pececito de colores (n) (m)
goldfish

pedal (n) (m)
pedal

pegajoso (adj)
sticky

pegatina (n) (f)
sticker

peine (n) (m)
comb

pelícano (n) (m)
pelican

película (n) (f)
movie

peligro (n) (m)
danger

peligroso (adj)
dangerous

pelo (n) (m)
hair

pelota (n) (f)
ball

peludo (adj)
hairy

peluquería (n) (f)
hair salon

pelvis (n) (f)
hipbone

peor (adj)
worst

pequeño (adj)
little, small

pera (n) (f)
pear

percha (n) (f)
coat hanger

perezoso (adj)
lazy

perfecto (adj)
perfect

periódico (n) (m)
newspaper

pero (conj)
but

perrito (n) (m)
puppy

perrito caliente (n) (m)
hot dog

perro (n) (m)
dog

perro pastor (n) (m)
sheepdog

persona (n) (f)
person

pesado (adj)
heavy

pestaña (n) (f)
eyelash

pez/peces (n) (m, sing/plu)
fish

piano (n) (m)
piano

picnic (n) (m)
picnic

pico (n) (m)
beak

pie (n) (m)
foot

piedra (n) (f)
stone

piel (n) (f)
skin; fur

pierna (n) (f)
leg (of person)

pieza (n) (f)
piece

pijama (n) (m)
pajamas

pila (n) (f)
battery

piloto (n) (m/f)
pilot

pimiento/pimienta (n) (m/f)
pepper

piña (n) (f)
pineapple; pinecone

pincel (n) (m)
paint brush

pingüino (n) (m)
penguin

pino (n) (m)
pine tree

pintura (n) (f)
painting

piscina (n) (f)
swimming pool

piso (n) (m)
floor (of a building)

piso de abajo (n) (m)
downstairs

pizarrón (n) (m)
blackboard

pizza (n) (f)
pizza

plancha (n) (f)
iron (clothes)

planeta (n) (m)
planet

plano (adj)
flat

planta (n) (f)
plant

plástico (adj)
plastic

plastilina (n) (f)
modelling clay

plata (n) (f)
silver

plataforma (n) (f)
platform

plátano (n) (m)
banana

plato (n) (m)
plate

playa (n) (f)
beach

pluma (n) (f)
pen; feather

plumier (n) (m)
pencil case

pobre (adj)
poor

poco profundo (adj)
shallow

policía (n) (f)
police

polilla (n) (f)
moth

pollito (n) (m)
chick

pollo (n) (m)
chicken

polo (n) (m)
pole

polución (n) (f)
pollution

polvo (n) (m)
powder; dust

popular (adj)
popular

por favor (adv)
please

por qué (adv)
why

por todos lados (adv)
everywhere

porque (conj)
because

posible (adj)
possible

postal (n) (f)
postcard

postre (n) (m)
dessert

pregunta (n) (f)
question

precio (n) (m)
price

premio (n) (m)
prize

presa (n) (f)
dam

presidente/presidenta (n) (m/f)
president

primavera (n) (f)
spring (season)

primero (adv)
first

primeros auxilios (n) (m)
first aid

primo/prima (n) (m/f)
cousin

princesa (n) (f)
princess

principal (adj)
main

príncipe (n) (m)
prince

problema (n) (m)
problem; trouble

probablemente (adv)
probably

producto lácteo (adj)
dairy

profundo (adj)
deep

programa (n) (m)
program

pronto (adv)
soon

propio (adj)
own

protector solar (n) (m)
sunblock

proyecto (n) (m)
project

prueba (n) (f)
quiz

pudin (n) (m)
pudding

pueblo (n) (m)
village

puente (n) (m)
bridge

puerta (n) (f)
door

puerta principal (n) (f)
front door

puerto (n) (m)
harbor

pulgar (n) (m)
thumb

pulsera (n) (f)
bracelet

puño (n) (m)
fist

puntaje (n) (m)
score

puntiagudo (adj)
pointed

punto (n) (m)
point

Q

querido (adj)
dear (in a letter)

queso (n) (m)
cheese

quien/quién/quienes/ quiénes (pron)
who

quieto (adj)
still

quizá/quizás (adv)
perhaps, maybe

R

radio (n) (f)
radio

raíz (n) (f)
root

rama (n) (f)
branch

rana (n) (f)
frog

rápido (adv)
fast

raqueta (n) (f)
racket

rascacielos (n) (m)
skyscraper

rastrillo (n) (m)
rake

rata (n) (f)
rat

ratón (n) (m)
mouse (animal); mouse (computer)

raya (n) (f)
stripe

real (adj)
real

realmente (adv)
really

receta (n) (f)
recipe

recibo (n) (m)
receipt

recreo (n) (m)
playtime; break

rectángulo (n) (m)
rectangle

recto (adj)
straight

recuerdo (n) (m)
souvenir

red (n) (f)
net

redondo (adj)
round

refrigerador (n) (m)
fridge

regadera (n) (f)
watering can

regalo (de cumpleaños) (n) (m)
(birthday) present

regla (n) (f)
ruler (measuring)

reina (n) (f)
queen

relámpago (n) (m)
lightning

reloj (n) (m)
clock; wristwatch

remo (n) (m)
oar

renacuajo (n) (m)
tadpole

reproductor de discos compactos (n) (m)
CD player

reproductor de DVD (n) (m)
DVD player

rescate (n) (m)
rescue

respuesta (n) (f)
answer

restaurante (n) (m)
restaurant

reto (n) (m)
challenge

revista (n) (f)
magazine

rey (n) (m)
king

rico (adj)
rich

rinoceronte (n) (m)
rhinoceros

río (n) (m)
river

rizado (adj)
curly

robot (n) (m)
robot

roca (n) (f)
rock

rodilla (n) (f)
knee

rojo (adj)
red

rompecabezas (n) (m)
puzzle

ropa (n) (f)
clothes

ropa interior (n) (f)
underwear

rosa (adj)
pink

rosa (n) (f)
rose

roto (adj)
broken

rubio (adj)
blonde

rueda (n) (f)
roundabout; wheel

rugby (n) (m)
rugby

rugoso (adj)
rough

ruidoso (adj)
noisy

ruta (n) (f)
route

S

sábana (n) (f)
sheet (on bed)

saco (n) (m)
sack

saco de dormir (n) (m)
sleeping bag

sal (n) (f)
salt

sala (n) (f)
living room

salario (n) (m)
pay

salida (n) (f)
exit

salón de clase (n) (m)
classroom

salvaje (adj)
wild

salvavidas (n) (m)
lifeguard

sandalia (n) (f)
sandal

sandía (n) (f)
watermelon

sándwich (n) (m)
sandwich

sangre (n) (f)
blood

sano (adj)
healthy

sapo (n) (m)
toad

sartén (n) (f)
frying pan

seco (adj)
dry

sediento (adj)
thirsty

segundo (adj)
second

seguro (adj)
safe; sure; certain

sello (n) (m)
stamp

selva tropical (n) (f)
rain forest

semáforo (n) (m)
traffic lights

semana (n) (f)
week

semanada (n) (f)
pocket money

semicírculo (n) (m)
semicircle

semilla (n) (f)
seed

señal (n) (f)
sign

sencillo (adj)
plain, simple

sendero (n) (m)
path

sentido (n) (m)
sense

serpiente (n) (f)
snake

servilleta de papel (n) (f)
paper towel

siempre (adv)
always

significado (n) (m)
meaning

siguiente (adj)
next

silbato (n) (m)
whistle

silencioso (adj)
quiet

silla (n) (f)
chair

silla de montar (n) (f)
saddle

silla de playa (n) (f)
deck chair

silla de ruedas (n) (f)
wheelchair

sillón (n) (m)
armchair

silvestre (adj)
wild

símbolo (n) (m)
symbol

sin (prep)
without

sin hacer ruido (adv)
quietly

sino (conj)
but

sitio web (n) (m)
Web site

snowboard (n) (m)
snowboard

sobre (n) (m)
envelope

sobre (prep)
about

sobrino/sobrina (n) (m/f)
nephew/niece

sofá (n) (m)
sofa

sol (n) (m)
sun

solamente (adv)
only

soldado (n) (m)
soldier

soleado (adj)
sunny

sólido (n) (m)
solid

solo (adj)
alone

sólo (adv)
just; only

sombra (n) (f)
shadow

sombrero (n) (m)
hat

sordo (adj)
deaf

sorprendente (adj)
surprising

sorpresa (n) (f)
surprise

sótano (n) (m)
basement

su (de él) (adj)
his

su (de ella) (adj)
her

su (de ello) (adj)
its

su/sus (adj) (sing/plu)
their

suave (adj)
gentle; smooth

suavemente (adv)
gently

submarino (n) (m)
submarine

subterráneo (adj)
underground

sucio (adj)
dirty

suelo (n) (m)
floor

suelto (adj)
loose

sueño (n) (m)
dream

suéter (n) (m)
sweater

suficiente (adj)
enough

superficie (n) (f)
surface

supermercado (n) (m)
supermarket

sur (n) (m)
south

suyo (de él) (pron)
his

suyo (de ella) (pron)
hers

T

tabla de surf (n) (f)
surfboard

tablero (n) (m)
board

tal vez (adv)
maybe

tallo (n) (m)
stem

tamaño (n) (m)
size

también (adv)
also; too

tambor (n) (m)
drum

tapa (n) (f)
lid

tapete (n) (m)
rug

tarde (adv)
late

tarde (n) (f)
evening

tarea (n) (f)
homework

tarjeta (n) (f)
card

taxi (n) (m)
taxi

taza (n) (f)
mug, cup

tazón (n) (m)
bowl

té (n) (m)
tea

techo (n) (m)
ceiling

teclado (n) (m)
keyboard

tejado (n) (m)
roof

tela (n) (f)
cloth

teléfono (n) (m)
phone

teléfono celular (n) (m)
cellular phone

telescopio (n) (m)
telescope

televisión (n) (f)
television

tempestuoso (adj)
stormy

temporada (n) (f)
season

temprano (adv)
early

tenedor (n) (m)
fork

tenis (n) (m)
tennis

tenis de mesa (n) (m)
table tennis

tercero (adj)
third

término (n) (m)
end; term

termómetro (n) (m)
thermometer

ternero (n) (m)
calf (animal)

terrible (adj)
terrible

tía (n) (f)
aunt

tiburón (n) (m)
shark

tiempo (n) (m)
time

tiempo (n) (m)
weather

tiempo libre (n) (m)
free time

tienda (n) (f)
shop

tienda de campaña (n) (f)
tent

tierra (n) (f)
land, ground; soil

Tierra (n) (f)
Earth (planet)

tigre (n) (m)
tiger

tijeras (n) (f)
scissors

timbre (n) (m)
bell

tímido (adj)
shy

tío (n) (m)
uncle

tipo (n) (m)
kind, type

toalla (n) (f)
towel

tobillo (n) (m)
ankle

todo (adj/pron)
all, everything

todo el mundo (pron)
everybody

tomate (n) (m)
tomato

tormenta (n) (f)
thunderstorm

tornado (n) (m)
tornado

tortuga (n) (f)
tortoise; turtle

tos (n) (f)
cough

tostadora (n) (f)
toaster

trabajo (n) (m)
job

tractor (n) (m)
tractor

tráfico (n) (m)
traffic

traje (n) (m)
suit

traje de baño (n) (m)
swimsuit

tranquilo (adj)
peaceful, quiet

transbordador (n) (m)
ferry

transporte (n) (m)
transport

tras (prep)
after

travieso (adj)
naughty

tren (n) (m)
train

tren eléctrico (n) (m)
train set

triángulo (n) (m)
triangle

trigo (n) (m)
wheat

trineo (n) (m)
sled, sleigh

tripulación (n) (f)
crew

triste (adj)
sad

trompa (n) (f)
trunk (of animal)

tronco (n) (m)
trunk (of tree)

tropical (adj)
tropical

tú (pron)
you

tubo (n) (m)
tube

tucán (n) (m)
toucan

túnel (n) (m)
tunnel

turista (n) (m)
tourist

U

ubicación (n) (f)
location

último (adj)
last

un/una (article) (m/f)
a, an

uña (n) (f)
nail

uniforme (n) (m)
uniform

uniforme escolar (n) (m)
school uniform

universidad (n) (f)
college

universo (n) (m)
universe

útil (adj)
useful

uva (n) (f)
grape

V

vaca (n) (f)
cow

vacaciones (n) (f)
vacation

vacío (adj)
empty

valiente (adj)
brave

vapor (n) (m)
steam

vaquero/vaquera (n) (m/f)
cowboy/cowgirl

vaqueros (n) (m)
jeans

varón (n) (m)
male

vaso (n) (m)
glass (drink)

vecino (n) (m)
neighbor

vegetariano/vegetariana (n) (m/f)
vegetarian

vela (n) (f)
candle; sail (of boat)

velero (n) (m)
sailboat

vendedor/vendedora (n) (m/f)
shopkeeper

ventana (n) (f)
window

verano (n) (m)
summer

verbo (n) (m)
verb

verde (adj)
green

verdura (n) (f)
vegetable

vestíbulo (n) (m)
hall

vestido (n) (m)
dress

veterinario/veterinaria (n) (m/f)
vet

viaje (n) (m)
trip, journey

vida (n) (f)
life

video (n) (m)
video player

videojuego (n) (m)
video game

viejo (adj)
old

viento (n) (m)
wind

violeta (adj)
purple

violín (n) (m)
violin

vosotros/vosotras (pron) (m/f, plu)
you

Y

y (conj)
and (except before i/hi)

ya (adv)
already

yo (pron)
I (pron)

yogur (n) (m)
yogurt

Z

zanahoria (n) (f)
carrot

zapatilla (n) (f)
slipper

zapatillas deportivas (n) (f)
sneakers

zapato (n) (m)
shoe

zona (n) (f)
zone

zoo (n) (m)
zoo

zorro (n) (m)
fox

zurdo (adj)
left-handed

Speaking Spanish

In this dictionary, we have spelled out each Spanish word in a way that will help you pronounce it. Use this guide to understand how the word should sound when you say it. Some parts of a word are shown in capital letters. These parts need to be stressed.

Spanish letter	Pronunciation	Our spelling	Example
a	like *a* in c*a*t	**a** or **ah**	**casa** *KA-sa*
e	like *ea* in h*ea*d	**e** or **eh**	**hermano** *air-MAH-noh*
i	like *e* in m*e*	**ai, ay** or **ee**	**comida** *ko-ME-da*
o	like *o* in h*o*le	**o** or **oh**	**pelota** *pay-LO-tah*
u	like *oo* in g*oo*d	**oo**	**música** *MOO-see-kah*
j	like *h* in *h*appy but rougher	**H**	**jabón** *Hah-BON*
g (ga, go, gu)	like *g* in *g*et	**g**	**gato** *gah-to*
g (ge, gi)	like *h* in *h*appy but rougher	**H**	**gente** *HEN-tay*
g (gue, gui)	like *g* in *g*et	**g**	**guerra** *GAY-rrah*
c (ca, co, cu)	like *c* in *c*at	**k**	**camino** *ka-ME-no*
c (e, i)	like *s* in *s*eat	**s**	**cebra** *SAY-bra*
qu	like *k* in *k*itten	**k**	**queso** *KAY-so*
ñ	like *ni* in o*ni*on	**n'y**	**niño** *NEE-n'yoh*
h	*h* is silent, except after "c"	**silent**	**hermana** *air-MAH-na*
ch	like *ch* in mu*ch*	**ch**	**mucho** *MOO-choh*
ll	like *lli* in mi*lli*on	**l'y**	**caballo** *kah-BAH-l'yo*

Verbs

This section gives a list of useful verbs (doing words). The most basic form of a verb (to …) is the infinitive. Useful verbs, such as "to be" *ser* and *estar* and "to have" *tener*, are written out so that you can see how they change depending on who is doing the action: I = yo; you = tú, usted; he/she = él/ella; we = nosotros/as; you (plural) = vosotros/as, ustedes; they = ellos/ellas.

In Spanish, you use the *usted* and *ustedes* forms of the verb when you want to be polite, especially with someone older than you.

Three of the most regular Spanish verbs are also written out: to speak = *hablar*, to eat = *comer*, and to live = *vivir*. There is a reflexive verb written out too. Reflexive verbs are often used where you would say "myself" or "yourself" in English, eg. to wash oneself = *lavarse*.

The verbs that are written out are shown in the present tense – they describe what is happening now or what you normally do.

---

to act
actuar
ack-too-AR

to agree
estar de acuerdo
ess-TAR deh ah-koo'ER-do

to ask
preguntar
preh-goon-TAR

to ask for
pedir
peh-DEER

to bake
hacer al horno
ah-SAIR ahl OR-no

to bark
ladrar
lah-DRAR

In Spanish there are two verbs for to be: *ser* and *estar*. *Ser* is used with your name, your profession, your nationality, and with descriptions; *estar* with positions and locations and to make the "ing" form of verbs.

to be
(permanent characteristic)
ser
sair

I am yo soy
you are tú eres
he, she, (you polite) is
él, ella, (usted) es
we are nosotros/nosotras somos
you are vosotros/vosotras sois
they, (you polite plural) are
ellos, ellas, (ustedes) son

---

to be (temporary quality)
estar
ess-STAR

I am yo estoy
you are tú estás
he, she, (you polite) is
él, ella, (usted) está
we are
nosotros/as estamos
you are
vosotros/as estáis
they, (you polite plural) are
ellos/ellas, (ustedes) están

to be able
poder
po-DAIR

to be born
nacer
NAH-sair

to be called
llamarse
yah-MAR-seh

Hago pasteles **al horno**.

Simón **muerde** una manzana.

Hincha un globo.

Luisa **lleva** las bolsas.

to be cold/hot
tener frío/calor
teh-NAIR FREE-o/kah-LOR

to be hungry
tener hambre
teh-NAIR AHM-breh

to be scared of
tener miedo de
teh-NAIR mee'EH-do deh

to be thirsty
tener sed
teh-NAIR sehd

to become
hacerse
ah-SAIR-seh

to begin
empezar
em-peh-SAR

to behave
comportarse
kom-por-TAR-seh

to believe
creer
kree-AIR

to bend
doblar
do-BLAR

to bird-watch
observar los pájaros
ob-sair-BAR loss PAH-Har-ross

to bite
morder
mor-DAIR

to blow up (a balloon)
hinchar (un globo)
in-CHAR

to borrow
tomar prestado
to-MAR press-TAH-do

to bounce
rebotar
reh-bo-TAR

to brake
frenar
freh-NAR

to break
romper
rom-PAIR

to breathe
respirar
rres-pee-RAR

to bring
traer
trah-AIR

to brush
cepillar
seh-pee-YAR

to brush one's teeth
cepillarse
los dientes
seh-pee-YAR-seh
los dee-EN-tehs

to build
construir
kons-troo-EER

to bump into
encontrarse
en-kon-TRAR-seh

to buy
comprar
kom-PRAR

to call
llamar
yah-MAR

to carry
llevar
yeh-BAR

to catch
coger
ko-HAIR

to cause
causar
kah'oo-SAR

to celebrate
celebrar
seh-leh-BRAR

to change
cambiar
kahm-BE'AR

to charge (a phone)
cargar
kar-GAR

to check
comprobar
kom-pro-BAR

to choose
elegir
eh-leh-HEER

Coge la pelota.

A B C D E F G H I J K L M N O P Q R S T U V W X Y Z

115

A
B
C
D
E
F
G
H
I
J
K
L
M
N
O
P
Q
R
S
T
U
V
W
X
Y
Z

to clean
limpiar
lim-PEE-AR

to clear
despejar
dess-peh-HAR

to climb
escalar
ess-kah-LAR

to close
cerrar
seh-RRAR

to collect
coleccionar
ko-lek-se'oh-NAHR

to come
venir
beh-NEER

to come back
volver
bol-BAIR

to come from
venir de
beh-NEER day

to compare
comparar
kom-pah-RAR

to complain
quejarse
keh-HAR-seh

to contain
contener
kon-teh-NAIR

to continue
continuar
kon-tee-noo-AR

to cook
cocinar
ko-si-NAR

to copy
copiar
ko-PEE-AR

to cost
costar
kos-TAR

to count
contar
kon-TAR

to cover
cubrir
koo-BREER

to crack
abrir
ah-BREER

to crash
chocar
cho-KAR

to create
crear
kreh-AR

to cross
cruzar
kroo-SAR

to cry
llorar
yo-RAR

to cut
cortar
kor-TAR

to cut out
recortar
reh-kor-TAR

to cycle
montar en bicicleta
mon-TAR en be-se-KLAY-tah

to dance
bailar
bah'e-LAR

to decide
decidir
deh-see-DEER

to decorate
decorar
deh-ko-RAR

to describe
describir
dess-kree-beer

*Cristina **baila** bien.*

*Ana **cava** en la arena.*

116

*Alberto **hace** el jardín.*

to die
morir
mo-REER

to dig
excavar
eks-kah-BAR

to disappear
desaparecer
dess-ah-pah-reh-SAIR

to discover
descubrir
dess-koo-BREER

to dive (from poolside)
tirarse de cabeza
tee-RAR-say day kah-BEH-sah

to do
hacer
ah-SAIR

I do yo hago
you do tú haces
he, she, (you polite) does
él, ella, (usted) hace
we do
nosotros/as hacemos
you do
vosotros/as hacéis
they, (you polite plural) do
ellos/ellas, (ustedes) hacen

to draw
dibujar
dee-boo-HAR

to dream
soñar
so-N'YAR

to dress up
disfrazarse
diss-frah-SAR-seh

to drink
beber
beh-BAIR

to drive
conducir
kon-doo-SEER

to dry
secar
seh-KAR

to earn
ganar
gah-NAR

to eat
comer
ko-MAIR

I eat yo como
you eat tú comes
he, she, (you polite) eats
él, ella, (usted) come
we eat
nosotros/as comemos
you eat
vosotros/as coméis
they, (you polite plural) eat
ellos/as, (ustedes) comen

to encourage
animar
ah-nee-MAR

*Yo **como** pastel de chocolate.*

to enjoy
disfrutar
diss-froo-TAR

to escape
escapar
ess-kah-PAR

to explain
explicar
eks-plee-KAR

to fall
caer
kah-AIR

to fall down
caerse
kah-AIR-seh

to feed
dar de comer
DAR day ko-MAIR

to feel
sentir
sen-TEER

to fetch
traer
trah-AIR

to fight
pelear
peh-leh-AR

to fill
llenar
yeh-NAR

to find
encontrar
en-kon-TRAR

*¡**Da de comer** a los perros!*

A B C D E F G H I J K L M N O P Q R S T U V W X Y Z

117

to find out
averiguar
ah-beh-ree-GOO'AR

to finish
terminar
ter-min-AR

to fit
caber
kah-BAIR

to float
flotar
flo-TAR

to fly
volar
bo-LAR

to fold
doblar
do-BLAR

to follow
seguir
seh-GHEER

to forget
olvidar
ol-be-DAR

to freeze
congelar
kon-Heh-LAR

to frighten
asustar
ah-soos-TAR

to garden
hacer el jardín
ah-SAIR el Har-DEEN

to get
obtener
ob-teh-NAIR

Dobla el papel.

to get on (a bus)
subirse
soo-beer-seh

to get ready
prepararse
preh-pah-RAR-seh

to get up
levantarse
le-ban-TAR-she

to give
dar
DAR

to go
ir
EER

I go yo voy
you go tú vas
he, she, (you polite) go
él, ella, (usted) va
we go nosotros/as vamos
you go vosotros/as váis
they, (you polite plural) go
ellos/ellas, (ustedes) van

to go camping
ir de acampada
EER day ah-cahm-pah-da

to go on vacation
ir de vacaciones
EER day bah-kah-si-O-nes

to go out
salir
sah-LEER

to go shopping
ir de compras
EER day KOM-pras

to grow
crecer
kreh-SAIR

to guess
adivinar
ah-dee-be-NAR

to hang up (phone)
colgar
kol-GAR

to happen
suceder
soo-seh-DAIR

to hate
odiar
o-DEE-AR

to have
tener
teh-NAIR

I have yo tengo
you have tú tienes
he, she, (you polite) has
él, ella, (usted) tiene
we have
nosotros/as tenemos
you have
vosotros/as tenéis
they, (you polite plural) have
ellos/ellas, (ustedes) tienen

to have a bath
bañarse
bah-N'YAH-seh

Carlos desayuna huevos.

María se está divirtiendo.

to have a shower
ducharse
doo-CHAR-seh

to have breakfast
desayunar
dess-ah-yoo-NAR

to have dinner
cenar
seh-NAR

to have fun
divertirse
dee-bair-TEER-seh

to hear
oír
o-EER

to help
ayudar
ah-yoo-DAR

to hide
esconder
ess-kon-DAIR

to hit
pegar
peh-GAR

to hold
sujetar
soo-He-TAR

to hop
dar saltos
DAR SAHL-tos

to hope
esperar
ess-peh-RAR

to hurry
darse prisa
dar-seh PREE-sah

to hurt (oneself)
hacerse daño
ah-SAIR-seh DAH-n'yo

to imagine
imaginar
ee-mah-He-NAR

to include
incluir
in-kloo-EER

to inspire
inspirar
ins-pee-RAR

to invent
inventar
in-ben-TAR

to invite
invitar
in-be-TAR

to join
unirse
oo-NEER-seh

to jump
saltar
sahl-TAR

to keep
mantener
mahn-teh-NAIR

to keep warm
abrigar
ah-bree-GAR

to kick
dar una patada
DAR OO-nah pah-TAH-dah

to kill
matar
mah-TAR

to kiss
besar
beh-SAR

to know
saber
sah-BAIR

to land (in a plane)
aterrizar
ah-te-rree-SAR

to last
durar
doo-RAR

to laugh
reírse
reh-EER-seh

to lead
dirigir
dee-ree-HEER

to learn
aprender
ah-pren-DAIR

to lie
mentir
men-TEER

Las ranas dan grandes saltos por el aire.

A B C D E F G H I J K L M N O P Q R S T U V W X Y Z

119

A B C D E F G H I J K L M N O P Q R S T U V W X Y Z

to lift
levantar
leh-bahn-TAR

to like
gustar
goos-TAR

to listen (to)
escuchar
ess-koo-CHAR

to live
vivir
be-BEER

I live yo vivo
you live tú vives
he, she, (you polite) lives
él, ella, (usted) vive
we live
nosotros/as vivimos
you live
vosotros/as vivís
they, (you polite plural) live
ellos/ellas, (ustedes) viven

to lock
cerrar con llave
say-RRAR kon L'YA-bay

to look
mirar
mee-RAR

to look for
buscar
boos-KAR

to lose
perder
pair-DAIR

*Juan **escucha** música.*

to love
querer
keh-RAIR

to make
hacer
ah-SAIR

to make a wish
pedir un deseo
peh-DEER oon deh-SEH-o

to make friends
hacer amigos
ah-SAIR ah-MEE-gos

to marry
casarse
kah-SAR-seh

to mean
querer decir
keh-RAIR deh-SEER

to measure
medir
meh-DEER

to meet
quedar con
keh-DAR kon

to mix
mezclar
mes-KLAR

to move
mover
mo-BAIR

to need
necesitar
neh-seh-see-TAR

*Eva **mira** cuidadosamente.*

*Rosa **abre** la puerta.*

to not feel well
encontrarse mal
en-kon-TRAR-seh mahl

to notice
notar
no-TAR

to offer
ofrecer
o-freh-SAIR

to open
abrir
ah-BREER

to own
tener
teh-NAIR

to pack
hacer la maleta
ah-SAIR lah mah-LEH-tah

to paint
pintar
pin-TAR

to pay
pagar
pah-GAR

to persuade
persuadir
pair-soo'ah-DEER

to pick up
recoger
rreh-ko-HAIR

to plan
planear
plahn-TAR

to plant
plantar
plah-neh-AR

to play
jugar
Hoo-GAR

to play an instrument
tocar un instrumento
to-KAR oon in-stroo-MEN-to

to point
apuntar
ah-poon-TAR

to pour
echar
eh-CHAR

to practice
practicar
prak-tee-KAR

to predict
predecir
preh-deh-SEER

to prefer
preferir
preh-feh-REER

to prepare
preparar
preh-pah-RAR

to press
prensar
pren-SAR

to pretend
pretender
preh-ten-DAIR

to print
imprimir
im-pree-MEER

to produce
producir
pro-doo-SEER

to program
programar
pro-grah-MAR

to promise
prometer
pro-meh-TER

to protect
proteger
pro-teh-HAIR

to provide
proporcionar
pro-por-see'o-NAR

to pull
tirar
tee-RAR

to push
empujar
em-poo-HAR

to put
poner
po-NAIR

to put away
guardar
goo'ar-DAR

to rain
llover
l'yo-BAIR

to reach
alcanzar
ahl-kahn-SAR

to read
leer
leh-AIR

to realize
darse cuenta
DAR-seh KOO'EN-tah

to recognize
reconocer
rreh-ko-no-SAIR

to refuse
rechazar
rreh-chah-SAR

¡Echa el agua con cuidado!

¿Puedes pintar un cuadro?

A B C D E F G H I J K L M N O P Q R S T U V W X Y Z

ABCDEFGHIJKLMNOPQRSTUVWXYZ

to relax
relajarse
rreh-lah-HAR-seh

to remain
quedar
keh-DAR

to remember
recordar
rreh-kor-DAR

to repair
reparar
rreh-pah-RAR

to rest
descansar
dess-kahn-SAR

to return
regresar
rreh-greh-SAR

to ride a bicycle
montar en bicicleta
mon-TAR en be-se-KLAY-tah

to ride a horse
montar a caballo
mon-TAR ah kah-BAH-l'yo

to roll
enrollar
en-ro-L'YAR

to rub
frotar
fro-TAR

to run
correr
kor-RRER

Pablo **corre** rápido.

to run after
perseguir
pair-seh-GEER

to save
ahorrar
ah-o-RRAR

to say
decir
deh-SEER

to score (a goal)
marcar
mar-KAR

to scratch
rascar
rahs-KAR

to search
buscar
boos-KAR

to see
ver
BAIR

to seem
parecer
pah-reh-SAIR

to sell
vender
ven-DAIR

to send
enviar
en-be-AR

to set the table
poner la mesa
po-NAIR lah MEH-sah

Raquel **lee** su libro.

to share
compartir
kom-par-TEER

to shine
brillar
bree-YAR

to shout
gritar
gree-TAR

to show
mostrar
moss-TRAR

to sing
cantar
kahn-TAR

to sit
estar sentado/a
ess-TAR sen-TAH-do/ah

to sit down
sentarse
sen-TAR-seh

to skate
patinar
pah-tee-NAR

Mónica **monta** a caballo.

to ski
esquiar
ess-kee-AR

to sleep
dormir
dor-MEER

to slide
resbalar
rress-ba-LAR

to slip
resbalar
rress-ba-LAR

to smell
oler
o-LAIR

to smile
sonreír
son-reh-EER

to snow
nevar
neh-BAR

to sound (like)
sonar (como)
so-NAR

Ángel está durmiendo.

to speak
hablar
ah-BLAR

I speak yo hablo
you speak tú hablas
he, she, (you polite) speaks
él, ella, (usted) habla
we speak
nosotros/as hablamos
you speak
vosotros/as habláis
they, (you polite plural) speak
ellos/ellas, ustedes hablan

to spell
deletrear
deh-leh-treh-AR

to spin
dar vueltas
DAR boo'EL-tahs

to spread
extender
eks-ten-DAIR

to stand
estar de pie
ess-TAR day PEE'EH

to stand up
ponerse de pie
po-NAIR-seh day PEE'EH

to start
empezar
em-peh-SAR

to stay
quedarse
keh-DAR-seh

*Lucía le **grita** a su amigo.*

to stick
pegar
peh-GAR

to sting
picar
pee-KAR

to stop
parar
pah-RAR

to stretch
estirar
ess-tee-RAR

to study
estudiar
ess-too-DEE'AR

to surf
hacer surf
ah-SAIR soorf

to surprise
sorprender
sor-pren-DAIR

to survive
sobrevivir
so-breh-be-BEER

to swim
nadar
nah-DAR

to take
tomar
to-MAR

*Marcia **extiende** el chocolate en los pasteles.*

A B C D E F G H I J K L M N O P Q R S T U V W X Y Z

to take photos • sacar fotos

La niña saca una foto.

to take photos
sacar fotos
sah-KAR FOH-toss

to take away
quitar
kee-TAR

to take care of
cuidar
koo'ee-DAR

to take turns
hacer turnos
ah-SAIR TOOR-nos

to talk
hablar
ah-BLAR

to tape
grabar
grah-BAR

to taste
probar
pro-BAR

to teach
enseñar
en-seh-N'YAR

to tease
tomar el pelo
to-MAR el PEH-lo

to tell
contar
kon-TAR

to tell a story
contar una historia
kon-TAR OO-nah iss-TOH-ree'ah

to tell the time
decir la hora
deh-SEER lah O-rah

to thank
agradecer
ah-grah-deh-SAIR

to think
pensar
pen-SAR

to throw
tirar
tee-RAR

to tie
atar
ah-TAR

to touch
tocar
to-KAR

to train
entrenar
en-treh-NAR

to translate
traducir
trah-doo-SEER

to travel
viajar
be'ah-HAR

to treat (well)
tratar (bien)
trah-TAR (BE'EN)

to try
intentar
in-ten-TAR

to try on
probar
pro-BAR

to turn
girar
Hee-RAR

to twist
enrollar
en-ro-L'YAR

to type
escribir a máquina
ess-kree-BEER ah MAH-kee-nah

to understand
entender
en-ten-DAIR

to undo
deshacer
dess-ah-SAIR

to undress
desnudarse
dess-noo-DAR-seh

to unpack
deshacer la maleta
dess-ah-SAIR
lah mah-LEH-tah

Tira el balón, Luis.

Isabel está pensando.

124

to use
usar
oo-SAR

to visit
visitar
be-see-TAR

to wait
esperar
ess-peh-RAR

to wake up
despertarse
dess-pair-TAR-seh

to walk
andar
ahn-DAR

to want
querer
keh-RAIR

I want yo quiero
you want tú quieres
he, she, (you polite) wants
él, ellas, (usted) quiere
we want
nosotros/as queremos
you want
vosotros/as queréis
they, (you polite plural) want
ellos, ellas, (ustedes) quieren

Jaime **escribe** un correo electrónico.

Laura **lava** los platos.

to warm
calentarse
kah-len-TAR-seh

to wash
lavar
lah-BAR

to wash (oneself)
lavarse
lah-BAH-seh

I wash myself
yo me lavo
you wash yourself
tú te lavas
**he, she, (you polite)
washes himself**
él, ellas, (usted) se lava
we wash ourselves
nosotros/as nos lavamos
you wash yourselves
vosotros/as os laváis
**they, (you polite plural)
wash themselves**
ellos/ellas, (ustedes) se lavan

to wash the dishes
lavar los platos
la-BAR los PLAH-tos

to watch
ver
BAIR

mirar
mee-RAR

to wave
saludar
sah-loo-DAR

to wear
llevar (puesto)
ye-BAR (poo'ESS-to)

to weigh
pesar
peh-SAR

to whisper
susurrar
soo-soor-RRAR

to win
ganar
gah-NAR

to wish
desear
deh-seh-AR

to wonder
preguntarse
preh-goon-TAR-seh

to work
trabajar
trah-bah-HAR

to work (function)
funcionar
foon-si'o-NAR

to wrap
envolver
en-bol-BAIR

to write
escribir
ess-kree-BEER

Eduardo **escribe** en su diario.

A B C D E F G H I J K L M N O P Q R S T U V W X Y Z

Useful phrases
Frases útiles

Learn the days of the week!

Monday
lunes
LOO-ness

Tuesday
martes
MAR-tess

Wednesday
miércoles
MEE'ER-koh-less

Thursday
jueves
HOO'EH-bess

Friday
viernes
BE'AIR-ness

Saturday
sábado
SAH-ba-doh

Sunday
domingo
do-MEEN-goh

yes
sí
see

no
no
no

hello
hola
O-lah

goodbye
adiós
a-DE'OS

see you later
hasta luego
AS-ta LOO'EH-go

please
por favor
POR fah-VOR

thank you
gracias
GRAH-se'ahs

excuse me
perdón
pair-DON

I'm sorry
lo siento
lo SEE'EN-toh

my name is…
me llamo…
meh L'YAH-moh

I live in…
vivo en…
BEE-bo en

I am…years old.
tengo…años.
TEN-goh…AH-n'yos

I don't understand
no comprendo
noh kom-PREN-doh

I don't know
no sé
no SEH

very well
muy bien
MOO'EE BE'EN

very much
mucho
MOO-choh

I do/don't like…
me/no me gusta…
meh/no meh GOOS-tah

Let's go!
¡Vamos!
BAH-moss

Happy birthday!
¡Feliz cumpleaños!
fay-LEES koom-play-AH-N'yos

Hola, me llamo Gabriel.

How are you?
¿Cómo estás?
KOH-moh es-TASS

What is your name?
¿Cómo te llamas?
KOH-moh tay yah-mas

Do you speak English?
¿Habla inglés?
ah-BLAH een-GLESS

Do you like...?
¿Te gusta...?
teh GOOS-ta

Do you have...?
¿Tienes...?
TE'EH-nes

Can I have...?
¿Me das...
meh DAS

How much...?
¿Cuánto...?
KOO'AHN-toh

What's that?
¿Qué es eso?
KEH ESS E-sso

How many...?
¿Cuántos/Cuantas...?
KOO'AHN-toss/KOO'AHN-tass

Can you help me?
¿Me puedes ayudar?
meh POO'EH-des a-yoo-DAR

What time is it?
¿Qué hora es?
KAY oh-ra ES

Help!
¡Socorro!
so-KOR-rro

Stop!
¡Para!
PAH-rah

turn right/left
gira a la derecha/
a la izquierda
*HEE-rah a lah day-RAY-chah/
a la ees-KE'AIR-dah*

go straight ahead
sigue recto
SEE-gay RREK-toh

in front of
delante de
day-LAHN-teh day

next to
al lado de
ahl LAH-do day

Where is/are...?
¿Dónde está/están...?
DON-deh es-TAH/es-TAHN

¡Vamos!

Learn the months of the year!

January
enero
en-NEH-roh

February
febrero
fe-BREH-roh

March
marzo
MAR-soh

April
abril
a-BREEL

May
mayo
MAY-yoh

June
junio
HOO-ne'oh

July
julio
HOO-le'oh

August
agosto
a-GOS-toh

September
septiembre
sep-TEE'EM-breh

October
octubre
ok-TOO-breh

November
noviembre
no-BEE'EM-breh

December
diciembre
dee-SEE'EM-breh

Useful phrases

Los números

Numbers

0 cero
seh-roh
zero

1 uno
OO-noh
one

2 dos
DOSS
two

3 tres
TRESS
three

4 cuatro
KOO'AH-troh
four

5 cinco
SEEN-koh
five

6 seis
SAYSS
six

7 siete
SEE-EH-teh
seven

8 ocho
O-choh
eight

9 nueve
NOO'EH-beh
nine

10 diez
DE'ES
ten

11 once
ON-seh
eleven

12 doce
DOH-seh
twelve

13 trece
TREH-seh
thirteen

14 catorce
ka-TOR-seh
fourteen

15 quince
KEEN-seh
fifteen

16 dieciséis
de'eh-see-SAYSS
sixteen

17 diecisiete
de'eh-see-SEE'EH-teh
seventeen

18 dieciocho
de'eh-see-O-cho
eighteen

19 diecinueve
de'eh-see-NOO'EH-beh
nineteen

20 veinte
BAYN-teh
twenty

21 veintiuno
bayn-tee-OO-noh
twenty-one

30 treinta
TRAYN-ta
thirty

40 cuarenta
koo'ah-REN-ta
forty

50 cincuenta
seen-KOO'EN-ta
fifty

60 sesenta
ses-SEN-ta
sixty

70 setenta
se-TEN-tah
seventy

80 ochenta
o-CHEN-ta
eighty

90 noventa
noh-BEN-ta
ninety

100 cien
SEE'EN
one hundred

Acknowledgments • Agradecimientos

DK would like to thank the following people: Sarah Ponder and Carole Oliver for design help; Marie Greenwood, Jennie Morris, Anna Harrison, and Lucy Heaver for editorial help; Angela Wilkes for language consultancy; Katherine Northam for digital artwork; Rose Horridge for picture research; Rachael Swann for picture research assistance; and Hope Annets, Mary Mead, Bethany Tombs, Todd and Sophie Yonwin for modelling.

The publisher would like to thank the following for their kind permission to reproduce their photographs: (Key: t = top, b = bottom, r = right, l = left, c = center)
31: www.aviationpictures.com/Austin J. Brown 1983 (tl); 31: Courtesy of FSTOP Pte. Ltd., Singapore (tc); 54: Corbis/Ronnie Kaufman (br); 55: Corbis/Craig Tuttle (tl); 55: Corbis/Craig Tuttle (tr); 55: Zefa/J. Jaemsen (cl);

55: Zefa/J. Jaemsen (cr); 55: Powerstock (bl); 72: Getty Images/Stone/Stuart Westmorland (tl); 82: Indianapolis Motor Speedway Foundation, Inc. (tc); 91: David Edge (tc); 91: Courtesy of Junior Department, Royal College of Music, London (br).
All other images © Dorling Kindersley.
For further information see
www.dkimages.com